Praise for *What Is the Church?*

"The author poses a big question, and he provides a grand answer. Using the rich threads of literature, historical events, Scripture and Tradition, and his lively Catholic faith, Regis Martin weaves a splendid tapestry that shows the beauty and the reality of Christ's Church. Like the Gospel, this book challenges us in our depths to receive the gift of God and to live it without compromise in the one 'place' where that is possible—His Church."

MOST REV. CHARLES J. CHAPUT, O.F.M. CAP., D.D.
Archbishop of Denver

"Regis Martin's sheer zest for the English language is only the first of the delights of this book. The reader finds himself drawn into a glorious and scholarly (never pedantic, always agile) encomium on the ancient Church, from a massively orthodox point of view (*Lumen Gentium* is Martin's principal text). An added delight is that Martin has read, quite simply, everything, and brings it all into vigorous play."

THOMAS HOWARD, PH.D.
Author, *On Being Catholic*

"In graduate school, I had the privilege of taking a theology class with Regis Martin on the Church. Regis did more than teach about the Church: he taught us why we should love the Church. In *What Is the Church?*, Dr. Martin shares this same vision with his readers. In a culture that does not understand Jesus Christ and His Bride, it is vitally important to have saints who understand and love them both."

CURTIS MARTIN
Founding President, Fellowship of Catholic University
Students (FOCUS)

"Regis Martin is himself a gift to the Church. He uses his manifold talents as theologian and teacher to lead his students, his readers, and his friends more deeply into the Christian mystery. He has taken the time, even in the midst of all that is demanded of a committed family man, to ponder more deeply on biblical, theological, and conciliar texts, and to follow the God-given truths wherever they will lead. He does this with a sensitivity and an elegance in writing that add to the joy.

"His new book, *What Is the Church?*, reflects all of these aspects of his life and work. In the face of the tens of thousands of pages which have been written in recent decades about the Second Vatican Council and what it 'really meant,' Dr. Martin takes a fresh and profound look at the Church's understanding, especially as it is expressed in *Lumen Gentium*.

"This is not a casual choice. As Dr. Martin states, 'If modern man wishes to understand himself completely, if he longs to overcome such blindness as prevents him from reaching his own Damascus, then he stands in need of Christ and His Church. Nowhere is the nature and mission of the Church more captivatingly put then in the premier conciliar document, *Lumen Gentium*, which lays bare the whole life and destiny of Christ's Bride and Body.'

"I do not hesitate to endorse and recommend this work, which is a genuine contribution to the emerging, more accurate understanding of the teaching and accomplishment of the Second Vatican Council."

MOST REV. JOHN J. MYERS, D.D., J.C.D.
Archbishop of Newark

"It is always a pleasure to see words dance on the page, animated by an author who loves to write and does it well. *What Is the Church?* is such a book, and Regis Martin is such a writer. We are amply supplied with stories of converts to the Catholic Church, but in this delightful book we have the confessions of a cradle Catholic. It is very much like sitting in front of a warm fire and listening to a great love story full of conversational moments and passionate insights. It is obvious that Regis Martin loves the Church and has loved her richly, for in this fine book he reveals his heart—and his rich intellect."

STEPHEN RAY
Author, *Crossing the Tiber*

"In his meditation on the mystery of the Church of Jesus Christ, Dr. Martin not only gives us deep and moving insights, but also clothes those insights in language both striking and beautiful. That is no surprise for those who know him. That is how he lectures and even talks, wordsmith that he is. His final tribute to our Blessed Mother is as eloquent as any I have read. If you read with a pencil in hand, have a sharpener handy when you read this book!"

REV. RAY RYLAND, J.D., PH.D.
Editor, *The Russian Church and the Papacy*
(by Vladimir Soloviev)

"Regis Martin has written a deeply theological, richly poetic meditation on the Church as we learn of her in that central document of the Second Vatican Council, *Lumen Gentium*. In an era of widespread ecclesiological confusion, *What Is the Church?* is filled with clarity, charity, and discernment. Dr. Martin wears his learning lightly and shares it beguilingly in a book that is at the same time light for the intellect and music for the soul."

RUSSELL B. SHAW
Author, *Papal Primacy in the Third Millennium*
and *Ministry or Apostolate?*

WHAT IS THE CHURCH?

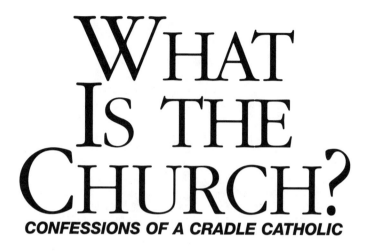

WHAT IS THE CHURCH?

CONFESSIONS OF A CRADLE CATHOLIC

EMMAUS ROAD
PUBLISHING
Steubenville, Ohio
A Division of Catholics United for the Faith

Regis Martin

Emmaus Road Publishing
827 North Fourth Street
Steubenville, Ohio 43952

Library of Congress Control Number: 2003102912
ISBN 1-931018-10-3

Cover design and layout by
Beth Hart

Cover artwork:
Velasquez, *Christ* (detail)

In honor of my father,
Regis E. Martin, Sr.,
a cradle Catholic eighty-four years
and counting.

"I love best of all that Church mud-splashed from history."
—*Jean Cardinal Daniélou, S.J.*

CONTENTS

CONTENTS

ABBREVIATIONS

Old Testament
Gen./Genesis
Ex./Exodus
Lev./Leviticus
Num./Numbers
Deut./Deuteronomy
Josh./Joshua
Judg./Judges
Ruth/Ruth
1 Sam./1 Samuel
2 Sam./2 Samuel
1 Kings/1 Kings
2 Kings/2 Kings
1 Chron./1 Chronicles
2 Chron./2 Chronicles
Ezra/Ezra
Neh./Nehemiah
Tob./Tobit
Jud./Judith
Esther/Esther
Job/Job
Ps./Psalms
Prov./Proverbs
Eccles./Ecclesiastes
Song/Song of Solomon
Wis./Wisdom
Sir./Sirach (Ecclesiasticus)
Is./Isaiah
Jer./Jeremiah
Lam./Lamentations

Bar./Baruch
Ezek./Ezekiel
Dan./Daniel
Hos./Hosea
Joel/Joel
Amos/Amos
Obad./Obadiah
Jon./Jonah
Mic./Micah
Nahum/Nahum
Hab./Habakkuk
Zeph./Zephaniah
Hag./Haggai
Zech./Zechariah
Mal./Malachi
1 Mac./1 Maccabees
2 Mac./2 Maccabees

New Testament
Mt./Matthew
Mk./Mark
Lk./Luke
Jn./John
Acts/Acts of the Apostles
Rom./Romans
1 Cor./1 Corinthians
2 Cor./2 Corinthians
Gal./Galatians
Eph./Ephesians
Phil./Philippians

Col./Colossians
1 Thess./1 Thessalonians
2 Thess./2 Thessalonians
1 Tim./1 Timothy
2 Tim./2 Timothy
Tit./Titus
Philem./Philemon
Heb./Hebrews
Jas./James
1 Pet./1 Peter
2 Pet./2 Peter
1 Jn./1 John
2 Jn./2 John
3 Jn./3 John
Jude/Jude
Rev./Revelation (Apocalypse)

FOREWORD

Man desperately needs the Church. She is there to guide, to teach, to make holy. The Church is a profound and mysterious link between the world and God. She provides a forum for an encounter with Christ. "For as His will is work, and this is named the world; so also His counsel is the salvation of men, and this has been called the church."[1]

The very fact that we breathe our next breath demands from us gratitude, since we are the recipients of the gift of being; indeed, if God did not actively will our being from one moment to the next, we would cease to be. But even more than that, our existence itself bespeaks a profound relationship between the Creator and us. God created us to love Him freely. How can one not be drawn to contemplate and marvel at our relationship with the Father? And in this contemplation of the Father, can we possibly avoid the urge to reflect on the mystery of our Redemption? At the heart of this mystery is the question, "What is the Church?"

In late November 1964, the fathers of the Second Vatican Council released the Dogmatic Constitution on the Church, *Lumen Gentium*. It was their intention to bring "the light of Christ to all men, a light brightly visible on the countenance of the Church." The result was a breathtaking examination of the "nature and universal

---

[1] Clement of Alexandria, *The Instructor*, in *Ante-Nicene Fathers*, vol. 2, ed. Alexander Roberts and James Donaldson (Peabody, Mass.: Hendrickson Publishers, 1994), bk. I, chap. iv.

mission" of the Church.[2] This document provides the backdrop for Dr. Regis Martin's profound reflections on the Church.

What better time to reflect on the nature and mission of the Church than now—almost forty years after *Lumen Gentium* was first published? The past forty years have no doubt been markedly chaotic as the clergy and laity have faced misunderstandings spread by those seeking to refashion the Church with human hands. There have been abuses and scandals on all fronts, but the Church is still the Church, and she continues to carry out her universal mission. She still conveys the light of Christ to humanity.

There is a tendency to reduce the Church to her buildings and to her hierarchical structures—to think of her as an "organization." But this book shatters such reductionism and opens the reader to a new understanding of the Church as that mystery which brings Christ to the world and thus conveys the holiness and nourishment we so need. The Church holds Christ high above her head as she trudges through the bog of human history.

As Dr. Martin points out, "At the heart of the Church, it is not *what* we find that matters, but *Who*, namely Christ, the Second Person of the Trinity, Who longs for an encounter with us in the sacrament which is His Church" (see p. 74-75). Without the Church we cannot have an encounter with Christ. What is this relational encounter if not faith? And how can this encounter possibly be made tangible? This is the heart of the mystery of the Church as a sacrament. She exists to make holiness tangible and to communicate this holiness to the world.

---

[2] Second Vatican Council, Dogmatic Constitution on the Church *Lumen Gentium* (November 21, 1964), no. 1.

What is striking about the mystery of the Church is that she is not only the bearer of Christ to the world, but also the very Body of Christ. What makes this scandalous is that in her members, she is not without blemish, but must constantly seek holiness and conversion. In the Church, even the saints are sinners and cry out to God for mercy. "It is the central paradox of her life, that she who dispenses the medicine of divine mercy is herself sorely in need of the same" (p. 73). To see the Church for what she truly is, one must have the eyes of faith, for she is not only visible, but also spiritual—not only human, but divine.

This series of reflections will deepen our faith and provide nourishment to our souls. Dr. Martin has a remarkable gift of being able to convey the truths of the faith in such a way as to evoke wonder at the beauty of the encounter with Christ. His manifest love for Catholic poetry and literature impresses upon his work an indelible beauty and grace.

Dr. Martin has a rare talent for stirring one's senses and bringing out the depth and grandeur of the Catholic faith. He invites us to leave the "boring pavement outside, free therefore to enter the mystery of her whom Christ Himself fashioned from His own pierced and crucified side as He hung upon the Cross to die" (p. 6). And so Dr. Martin will lead us into the heart of the Church, revealing the hidden truths that one can see only from within. Keep reading, and prepare to be swept off your feet by this most profound and strikingly beautiful book.

MICHAEL SULLIVAN

Editor, *Lay Witness*

INTRODUCTION

The first time I ever laid eyes on Rome was more than twenty years and half as many children ago. It was an entirely unforgettable affair. In fact, it was my clever wife who sent me over, as I myself did not have the presence of mind to think of it. She had at last persuaded me to finish off my studies in sacred theology at the Angelicum, a charming institution where (I was told) a young Polish priest by the name of Karol Wojtyla had once studied; and so one fine day I flew over to find a place to put my family up for the next couple of years, whilst I would slip away each day to study at the feet of learned Dominicans.

I remember that it was dreadfully hot that week in June. I wandered about Rome in a sort of daze, haplessly looking for an apartment. The noise and the dirt, I recall, were especially unnerving, as were the Gypsies, who seemed preternaturally bent on taking my money. And after five full days fruitlessly spent traipsing about the city, I'd come up completely empty. Perhaps, I began to ask myself, Rome wasn't all my clever wife had cracked it up to be. The allure of Rome, all the guidebooks assured me, was akin to that of being in love. But I was already in love, and all this, well, it was fast becoming loathsome. Maybe the magic *had* gone out of the place, and it was time now to cut bait, as they say, and return to the old U.S. of A., where there were plenty of graduate schools offering degrees in theology.

So there I was on the final day of my stay, the flight home was hours away, and desperation was clearly in the air. Not only had I not found a place to live—the existence of affordable apartments having eluded my efforts all week—but by now the heat and the noise and the dirt had quite unhinged me, not to mention a surfeit of screaming Italians, thieving Gypsies, and a bad case of jet lag. Was it—I kept asking myself—all for naught, the whole thing a washout?

It was then that I saw it. *It. Santa Maria della Vittoria.* Oh, what a splendid, serendipitous discovery it would prove to be! Raised up in honor of our blessed Lady, thanks to whose timely intercession at Lepanto a smashing victory had been won against the bloody Turk (it had been the decisive battle securing the safety of the Christian West), it fairly beckoned me to enter. And I had remembered Chesterton, too, who, in an inspired poem which every Catholic schoolboy once knew, had rhapsodized at great and memorable length about the courage of John of Austria, who, leading the charge against the sultan holding hostage countless Christian captives, had smashed the crescent which threatened even Rome herself. But it was Mary who had really won the great victory, scattering to the four winds the enemies of the true Church.

Of course, that was all in the distant past, more than four dead centuries ago. What had any of that to do with a tired man perspiring copiously along the pavement? Besides, not a whisper of that wonderment or grandeur appeared on the facade of her Church; like much of Rome's architecture, it was covered with the accumulated dust and soot of the centuries. Automobile exhaust had not helped much either. But I was tired and hot, and the noise of the city drove me inside, where, in a sudden swoon of astonishment, I beheld one of the greatest pieces of sculpture the world has ever seen. It took my breath completely away, for there, square in front of me, amid the silence of an interior wholly withdrawn from the world, stood Bernini's magnificent figure, *The Ecstasy of Saint Teresa.*

What the inspired Bernini had succeeded in rendering was the profoundest moment of Teresa's life, when an angel possessed of a flaming golden arrow repeatedly pierced her heart with the love of Christ. "The pain was so great," she writes in her autobiography, "that it made me moan, and the sweetness this greatest pain caused me was so superabundant that there is no desire capable of taking it away; nor is the soul content with less than God."[1]

I too felt the arrow, thrust however vicariously four centuries later by Gianlorenzo Bernini, the baroque genius whose works would prove so enrapturing during the time of my stay in the Eternal City. How often I would wander from the superb Piazza Navona with its fountain of four great rivers, an immense Egyptian obelisk lifted effortlessly above its center, across the Ponte Sant'Angelo with its formidable array of angels sculpted in purest marble, to the vast Square of Saint Peter's itself, its resplendent colonnade reaching out to embrace the pilgrim who has come home to Rome and to God.

In point of fact, I soon came to see that everything about the baroque conspires to awaken the senses, giving off a sheer panoply of sound and shape and color to play upon the window of the soul, and thus lead a man into the heart of the Church, the heart of Christ. I can still vividly recall my old friend and mentor, Fritz Wilhelmsen, surely the finest teacher I ever had, who first introduced me to the poetry of the transcendent, passionately declaiming on the subject of the baroque, insisting that it was never a mere symbol of

---

[1] Saint Teresa of Avila, *The Book of Her Life*, in *The Collected Works of St. Teresa of Avila*, vol. 1 (Washington: ICS Publications, 1976), 252.

anything. Rather, he said, it was "an explosion of reality," which moves a man immediately and dramatically to a confrontation with the living God. "The final test of the baroque," he would exclaim, his arms waving in a gesture of purest Catholic defiance, "is that no artistic snob can bear it. Its final tribute is that no Puritan can worship surrounded by the trappings of its spirit."

That is what Bernini did for me that afternoon in Rome. He made me see, by the sheer demonstration of Teresa's ecstatic state—her soul's rapture—the immense, joyous possibilities of life in Rome, a life surrounded by, immersed in, the things of God. Having seen, I resolved at once to stay. I never looked back on that day, with its sudden and felicitous, yet strangely unforeseen discovery, with the slightest regret. The sweetness and sorrow of that first week would, by turns, come to shape the contours of all our days in Rome.

The truth of anything, the poet Goethe tells us, whether it be art or friendship, God or the Church, is very like an encounter with stained glass: To see it properly, whole and entire, you have got to enter into the thing itself, seeing it from the angle of the one who gave it form, weight, extension. What he means, I think, is that you have got to leave the safety of the pavement outside, where it can only appear dull and dark and unwelcoming, and entering bravely into that space within, risk being struck dumb by the sudden dazzling disclosure of so much grace, clarity, beauty and proportion, qualities which irradiate the thing in all its richness and profundity.

Isn't this, really, the only way to the heart of the Church herself, whose *still point* (to use the image of T. S. Eliot I am most drawn to) will not be found along the pavement outside, from which perspective the view would only be pallid and prosaic? No, you have got to allow yourself to be drawn into the Church herself, to that light and life whence cometh our salvation. "At the still point of the turning world," writes Eliot, "there the dance is . . . and there is only the dance."[2]

It is to this end, dear reader, that I would hope to direct your attention in these pages, circling again and again round the one question that most matters. It is a question around which an entire conciliar event organized itself forty years ago, that is, the Second Vatican Council (1962-65). It framed that question in a more singular and radical way, moreover, than any Church gathering before: *What is the Church?* Or, to put it in scandalously precise terms: *Who is the Church?*

Where exactly does she belong in the great scheme of the world's salvation? Is she strictly necessary to our salvation? Or is she, as many so-called enlightened folk believe, only an externalization of ideas otherwise available to clever chaps like themselves? In the story of Saint Paul's conversion, the famous episode of God unhorsing him on his way to Damascus, so wonderfully depicted by the artist Murillo in a painting I once saw hanging in El Prado (in Madrid), there is one very piquant detail which has always impressed me. No sooner is he knocked to the ground and thereupon blinded by the light of heaven, than the voice of Jesus is asking, "[W]hy do you persecute me?" (Acts 9:4), as if He, Christ our Lord, were identifying Himself with those whom Saul had sought to torment and destroy. But in order for the blindness to be lifted, he must make his way to Damascus and there await the ministration of Ananias, leader of the Christian community, who will thus baptize and incorporate him into

---

[2] T. S. Eliot, *Four Quartets*, in *The Complete Poems and Plays: 1909-1950* (New York: Harcourt, Brace & World, 1971), 119.

Christ's Body, the Church. Where do we put the Church in the plan of God? Ask Saint Paul, for heaven's sake, who, despite God's pitching him onto the ground, and God's voice speaking to him, must nevertheless submit to human mediation in order to effect both his own cure and his subsequent commission as Apostle to the Gentiles.

Is not the point here about as plain as an Idaho potato? If modern man wishes to understand himself completely, if he longs to overcome such blindness as prevents him from reaching his own Damascus, then he stands in need of Christ and His Church. Nowhere is the nature and mission of that Church, of her profound and necessary connection to Christ, more captivatingly put than in the premier conciliar document itself, *Lumen Gentium*, which lays bare the whole life and destiny of Christ's Bride and Body. It is the text on which I wish especially to draw in these reflections, the text whose character and complexity I hope to examine. Won't you join me in this quest? Let us, together, leave behind the boring pavement outside, free therefore to enter the mystery of her whom Christ Himself fashioned from His own pierced and crucified side as He hung upon the Cross to die.

CHAPTER I

THE COURTESY OWED GOD

Years ago, a fellow by the name of Murray Kempton, a writer whose wonderfully ornate essays I have long admired, said that if you really wanted to capture your reader's attention, arresting his eye straightway, then you'd better set out to slay him with your opening sentence. Of course, he warned, if you do that, you run the risk of actually succeeding. What, I'd like to know, can be the advantage of wiping out your readership at one stroke?

Nevertheless, the point survives Murray's obvious exaggeration of it. On the other hand, even when you've got your reader firmly fastened to the page, there are still the usual second act problems: for instance, holding his attention for the duration of the story. This can be infuriatingly difficult, I have found, in the classroom, where the attention span of your average undergraduate tends not to be terribly high to begin with. Was it Mark Twain who said that few people were ever saved after the first ten minutes of a sermon? In the case of students, after the first ten minutes, they may not even be awake. The challenge of trying to reach young people these days, their minds encased in near catatonic slumber, may be likened to a stroll through a tree-lined cemetery: row upon row of unresponsive stones. No doubt this accounts for the reason why Generation X, weaned for the most part on perfectly vile music and movies—media in which the shrillest and most scabrous of sounds and images abound—is not likely to hang around for the second course of a meal which, let's face it, compared to the junk food found on the tube, consists only of words. After a minute or so in the company of even the most manic of verbalists (Robin Williams, say, catechizing David Letterman on the processions within the Godhead), the eyes predictably begin to glaze. Just take a minute to scan the faces of the usual Sunday Mass crowd the moment poor Father mounts the lectern to speak the Word. "There is no place where faces are so expressionless as in church during a sermon,"[1] wrote François Mauriac, who must have endured a great many, living as long as he did.

So every word has really got to count. Like Waterford Crystal, one cannot be too sparing. "A word is not the same with one writer as with another," Charles Péguy reminds us. "One tears it from his guts. The other pulls it out of his overcoat pocket."[2] I sometimes wonder if I—or anybody else for that matter—am quite sparing enough. Who, in fact, is ever equal to the job? Péguy? Yes, most certainly. I see him painfully wrenching each word from a heart broken on the wheel of an uncomprehending world, a world whose accelerating descent into a barbarism without Christ, a vast technocracy organized without reference to Him, he foretold in the months and years leading up to his

---

[1] François Mauriac, quoted in Antonio Socci, "Calendar: November 22, Saint Cecilia," *30 Days in the Church and the World*, no. 11 (November 1993): 74.

[2] One of many epigrams attributed to an astonishing writer and poet of Catholic France, the burden of whose sufferings and witness in the first years of the last century remain, alas, largely unremembered. For a wonderful compilation of his thought see Charles Péguy, *Temporal and Eternal*, trans. Alexander Dru (New York: Harper, 1958), recently reissued by the Liberty Fund (Indianapolis: Liberty Fund, 2001). See, in addition, his *The Portal of the Mystery of Hope*, trans. David Louis Schindler, Jr. (Grand Rapids: Wm. B. Eerdmans, 1996), an example of sheer unsurpassed poetry in which the broken human heart may regain something of that wholeness and healing God intended for man by His Son's descent.

death on the western front. Still, one has got to make the effort. To speak or write those luminous and galvanic sentences that can suddenly awaken the mind of a sophomore to life—what could be more satisfying to a teacher? It is on the order of finding a new planet, or savoring a heretofore undiscovered sensual pleasure. For a teacher there is nothing quite like the joy of accosting a roomful of twenty-something solipsists with one of those questions that, to quote Pascal, suddenly takes us by the throat. Who am I? Why am I here? Where am I going? To ask such questions is really at the heart of what teaching is about, which is giving witness to the truth, to that deepest of human longings to know and to love the truth. To throw light along the path leading to the God Who is Truth— what could be more satisfying?

So where does one start? Perched behind one's little podium, the feet carefully positioned some discreet distance from the forty or so humanoids staring across the divide, how does one begin? The important thing, of course, is to try to "force the moment to its crisis."[3] You have got to awaken the soul, unclog the cholesterol, get the juices going—which is what I aim to do every semester with a single cauterizing sentence from Romano Guardini, one of those nearly forgotten giants from the preconciliar past, a handful of whose books could spark a great renascence in Catholic life and thought. Guardini used to say that those who do not speak to God have nothing, nothing at all, to say to the world. Now isn't that an icebreaker? Because conversation with God is the highest and most important occupation known to man, not to engage in it—disdaining

---

[3] T. S. Eliot, "The Love Song of J. Alfred Prufrock," in *The Complete Poems and Plays: 1909-1950* (New York: Harcourt, Brace & World, 1971), 6.

even the acknowledgement that here is something important—is to stand completely mute before the world, evincing the most blithering imbecility about the things that matter.

Prayer is an absolutely universal human vocation. And, of course, what is given to man to do, indeed, God having inscribed our nature with such deeply felt necessity as to want to transcend it, must be within the reach of all men to do. Thus, even pagans pray (perhaps pagans especially, who inhabit a world suffused with a sense of the divine). Tacitus, the great Roman historian, in puzzling over the nature of the city, fixed on the fact that it was the temples of the gods and not the walls or the emperor that constituted its enduring and essential life. Monsignor Luigi Giussani, founder of one of Catholicism's most vibrant movements, Communion and Liberation, has described prayer as "the only human gesture which totally realizes the human being's stature."[4] Isn't this why we ascribe to Mary, the Mother of God, so exemplary an expression of that basic humanity? Who more than Mary, her arms outstretched and open to God, reveals, by the sheer transparence of her being before God, the most radical and perfect realization of what it means to be a creature?

But getting back to Guardini, what a lapidary line with which to launch a new course! A warhead hurled like that could serve at once to arrest the attention of all but the most otiose—at least among believers, that is, for whom prayer before class is not seen as an unwarranted breach of

---

[4] "To be conscious of oneself right to the core is to perceive, at the depths of the self, an Other. This is prayer: to be conscious of oneself to the very centre, to the point of meeting an Other. Thus prayer is the only human gesture which totally realizes the human being's stature." Rev. Msgr. Luigi Giussani, *The Religious Sense* (Montreal: McGrill-Queens University Press, 1997), 106.

the U.S. Constitution. As for those of atheist persuasion, the androids, I punish by telling them to offer it all up. It will, I assure them with mock solemnity, do their souls no end of good.

But what is this "talking to God" business, anyway? Prayer must seem such a quaint notion to folks moving briskly along the information superhighway. Armed with headsets and cell phones, have they really got time to punch in God's number? Have they even got time to be quiet? My sense is that people find silence positively unsettling. Even pious churchgoers tend to get a wee bit nervous when the music stops, after Communion, say, when the rubrics actually allow for a spot of silence, and they commence to fidget, so accustomed have their sensibilities become to that ambient noise in which we all live and move and (dis)locate our being. For others, I suspect, it amounts to an affront against the sacred democratic din that has come to dominate so much of modern life. Eliot calls it:

> The endless cycle of idea and action,
> Endless invention, endless experiment,
> Brings knowledge of motion, but not of stillness;
> Knowledge of speech, but not of silence;
> Knowledge of words, and ignorance of the Word.[5]

That special stillness which surrounds and fills everything beautiful and noble, which pervades especially the sacred, the numinous, is threatened as never before by the noise of words. "If someone were to ask me what the

---

[5] Eliot, "Choruses from 'The Rock,'" in *The Complete Poems and Plays*, 96.

liturgical life begins with," writes Guardini, "I should answer: with learning stillness. Without it, everything remains superficial, vain."[6]

This is why I so resist the impulse of telling my students very much on the first day. Of course, it may also reflect a certain pious deference to my Dominican masters from the Angelicum, where the sacred custom of *lectio brevis* (a short reading) held sway on opening day. Dismissing us after some blessedly few minutes, we would all repair to the nearest cappuccino bar for narcotic relief, accompanied by ritual expressions of gratitude for a tradition the violation of which would probably have brought down the institution. Of course, in Steubenville there are no cappuccino bars, although I note that the absence has not impeded my students any in finding their way out the door.

However, apart from not wishing to break with a beloved custom, I am also resistant to talk so much at the beginning because I have become rightly suspicious of people who feel the need to tell me everything they know, or show me all that they own, in the first twenty minutes. It suggests that perhaps they really don't know very much, nor have they got very much; but this, I allow, may be the result of a somewhat cynical turn of mind. Maybe I've just been to too many faculty meetings. Nevertheless, I like to remind my students that, after all, this is only the courtship phase and, who knows, maybe neither one of us will want to get married.

In his book *The World of Silence*, a deeply wise work that anyone who traffics in words ought to be made to read, Max Picard has written: "Silence provides a natural source of re-creation for language, a source of refreshment and

---

6 Rev. Romano Guardini, *Meditations before Mass* (Westminster, Md.: Newman Press, 1956), 6.

purification from the wickedness to which language itself has given rise. In silence language holds its breath and fills its lungs with pure and original air."[7]

Imagine if politicians, hot on the campaign trail, were to institute such a practice. In fact, says Picard, whenever two people come together to speak, there is always a third who listens. His name is Silence. It is as if, Picard tells us, "everything said here aloud in words has already happened in silence, for that is what gives the words their quality of sure certainty, intimacy, and sublimity."[8]

A little Picard goes a long way, I have found. It puts me in mind of Pascal's wry prediction, set down in the *Pensées*, that most of the crime committed in the world is the unhappy outcome of people unable to spend five minutes alone in their rooms. Hell, in other words, is not other people (Sartre was dead wrong there). Hell is being alone, and not just for five minutes, but forever.

So when the Psalmist says, "Today if you hear the voice of the Lord, harden not your hearts,"[9] what are we to make of it? In a world swept free of stillness, where the only voice we hear is our own, a mindless twittering amid the larger dissonance of radio and TV, how does one manage to keep *His* voice from becoming unheard and unheeded?

Often in trying to get a fix on the importance of putting prayer first, even in the classroom, I like to recall an observation I came across years ago, that it was God Himself Who instituted prayer in order to confer upon His creatures the dignity of becoming causes—an imperishable insight, it

---

[7] Max Picard, *The World of Silence* (Washington: Regnery Gateway, 1988), 38.

[8] *The World of Silence*, 39.

[9] Antiphon for the invitatory, Lenten Season, from *The Liturgy of the Hours*.

seems to me, and one especially worth passing along to impatient youth, for whom so often questions of empowerment get reduced to the political—that is, Who gets to do what to whom?—a question no more stultifying than which can scarcely be imagined. Meanwhile, how exquisitely simple is the truth before us: that by our prayers we literally cause things to happen, like, for instance, the success of one's study, or of this book. And isn't that, after all, the sense we are to assign the Lord's Prayer, the most celebrated petition ever lifted up before God? How instructive that Christ Himself, when asked by His apostles to pass on His practice of prayer, should enjoin them to ask the Father in heaven for this and that? Why not, then, I tell my students, importune God to help you learn to plumb the depths of the mystery of His Bride, the Church? Will God be disposed to help any of us if we don't take the time to ask? As Saint Alphonsus Liguori tells us in an extraordinary passage, approvingly set down in the Catechism: "Those who pray are certainly saved; those who do not pray are certainly damned."[10] Another icebreaker.

There is a devilish sort of penury, I am convinced, the very worst there is, when man is left to his own devices, when by sheer Promethean perversity he chooses to construct his own salvation, thus divesting himself of the generosity of God. (We are all, says Plato, children of poverty, that is, dependent upon the grace of God.) What else, then, is prayer but a willingness to tap into that inexhaustible supply? How thoughtful of Him to allow us freely to draw upon His own reservoir, the energy and strength of which sustain the whole universe. The world will be saved,

---

[10] Saint Alphonsus Liguori, *Del gran mezzo della preghiera*, in *Catechism*, no. 2744.

not by politics, but by prayer. Péguy, then, was right: When we collapse *mystique* into *politique*, reducing the things of God to the cheap coin of the secular realm, what someone has called "a Starbucks Catholicism in a Church mellow," the world will very soon spot the phoniness of it all, turning disgustedly away from a Church which obviously has nothing distinctive to offer. The category of the lapsed Catholic, I am told, amounts to the second largest denomination in the country, but would anyone in his right mind go to the wall defending so vapid an option? It is prayer on which we absolutely depend, because without it, without the life of grace it quickens, you and I are less than zero.

In thinking of prayer, of its importance in the life of God's People, including especially those I teach, I remember Cardinal Daniélou's searching comment that "If God exists, how can anything exist outside God, since the fullness of existence is exhausted once and for all in Him?"[11] Here sounds that wonderful metaphysical tocsin, whose theme is the necessary contingence of all created reality. Again, Cardinal Daniélou has the sense of it when he writes, "God's existence does not destroy my existence, but only stops my appropriation of my existence. It enjoins me to acknowledge it as received, from each instant to the next."[12] What a breathtaking proposition that is, inviting no less an entire ontology to be built upon its central premise, the judgment that all being remains rooted in God, Whose very name bespeaks Being ("I AM WHO I AM" [Ex. 3:14], to quote the shattering theophany of Mount Sinai, the summit surely of Old Testament theology). Each of us, as it were, is

---

[11] Jean Cardinal Daniélou, S.J., *The Scandal of Truth*, trans. W. J. Kerrigan (Baltimore: Helicon Press, 1962), 67.
[12] *The Scandal of Truth*, 67.

a word spoken by Another, without Whom we could not speak at all—indeed, could not even be. And so long as I speak the lines scripted from all eternity for me, lacking which my own speech reduces to incoherence—refusing, that is, to appropriate them as my own—then my voice is free to soar as high as heaven itself, whence cometh that Word Which is my salvation. Just think of it, I tell my students (coaxing their minds to the metaphysical): so many examples of nothingness brought into being, hovering forever above an abyss of purest nullity, yet everywhere sustained by Omnipotent Love Itself.

And the point of all this, I ask? Why, to move my students to solicit God in assisting their poor professor to teach them! Entirely self-serving, to be sure, but how else am I to impart the beauty and truth of the Church's life? If God writes straight with crooked lines, to recall that splendid Portuguese proverb, why can't this poor pretzel of mine be the chosen instrument for all that God wants them to learn? "Did you think God hadn't a sense of humor?" I ask. "Did you think I could do all this by myself?"

Here, finally, is the courtesy we owe to God, which courtesy (I insist) is extended the moment we raise our minds and hearts to Him. We are to ask God, in Christ, not merely to uphold our lives, helping us to live for Him ("Youth," a wise old man once said, "was not made for pleasure; youth was made for heroism"), but also to deepen our understanding, which needs to be steeped in the very wisdom and holiness of One Who remains the true architect of the Church, having rescued her from a life of harlotry amid the fleshpots of Egypt and Babylon. "[A]part from me," He tells the disciples, "you can do nothing" (Jn. 15:5).

So much for the presumption of prayer, which needs to undergird any effort to understand the nature of the Church.

In fact, the understanding presupposes the prayer; one cannot forego the appeal to God for help—otherwise, of course, mere human help will not avail. It is one of those givens we must take as a matter of course; if we leave it out, nothing happens, the engine collapses for want of fuel. But there are others, too, which need a bit of attention before plunging headlong into the question, What (Who) is the Church? These will be taken up in the next two chapters.

CHAPTER II

THE COURTESY OWED THE AUTHOR

I wish to speak here of a couple of things, which I think necessary to doing Catholic theology well, especially where it confronts the fact and mystery of the Church. These are matters that, unless attended to straightaway like low oil in a crankcase, constrain one to spend an awful lot of time spinning one's wheels in the study, while faith itself, like elusive dwellers of the desert, slips silently away.

What do I mean? Well, the very first thing we all must do (as I tried to set down in the first chapter) is make time for God. Let each day begin and end with Him. The world and all that is in it derive from God—nothing is, which He does not suffer to be—so every breath we take, every brush we make, ought to take account of that fact. It is the merest courtesy we owe to God. I like how the poet Hopkins puts it:

> Thee, God, I come from, to thee go,
> All day long I like fountain flow
> From thy hand out, swayed about
> Mote-like in thy mighty glow.
>
> What I know of thee I bless,
> As acknowledging thy stress
> On my being and as seeing
> Something of thy holiness.[1]

---

[1] Rev. Gerard Manley Hopkins, S.J., "'Thee, God, I come from, to thee go,'" in *The Poems of Gerard Manley Hopkins*, 4th ed. (London: Oxford University Press, 1967), 194.

Why *should* God stoop to assist us in understanding His mysteries, mysteries that aim to enter the very marrow of theology itself, if we never bother to ask Him? "Not for a single moment," writes Hans Urs von Balthasar, "can theology forget its roots from which all its nourishment is drawn: adoration, in which we see, in faith, the heavens opened; and obedience in living, which frees us to understand the truth"[2]—it plainly will not work without prayer, time for which is an absolute necessity for those determined to do the discipline.

"We must remember God more often than we draw breath,"[3] observes Saint Gregory of Nazianzus. I believe he means by that "all the time." And another saint, a doctor of the Church no less, Alphonsus Liguori, has already told us in a most refreshing and apodictic way what follows for those who will or will not remember. If you've prayed, you're saved. Those who don't, won't. Period.

Of course, one would perhaps wish to know how he knows this, but no doubt that is why Alphonsus is a saint and I (and possibly you, too, dear reader) are not—at least, not yet. "Sanctity," to quote a wise and witty priest of my acquaintance (long-suffering, too, since I have frequently inflicted my sins upon him), "sanctity consists in the struggle." And maybe we've yet to struggle to the point of shedding blood (cf. Heb. 12:4). That could change at any moment, I realize; the perilous state of the universe forbids all forms of Pickwickianism, especially with so many forces arrayed against the Church. Besides, whoever said the threat of torture and death, or even the merest

---

[2] Rev. Hans Urs von Balthasar, *Explorations in Theology: The Word Made Flesh* (San Francisco: Ignatius Press, 1989), 154.

[3] Saint Gregory of Nazianzus, *Orationes theologicae*, 27, 1, 4, in *Catechism*, no. 2697.

whisper of scorn and ridicule, were somehow tangential to being a Christian?

I so admire Balthasar's formulation, set down in his little book, *The Moment of Christian Witness*, because coming as it did amid the vaporous optimism of the late 1960s, it perfectly punctures that inane and ridiculous age. "[P]ersecution," he wrote then, "constitutes the normal condition of the Church in her relation to the world, and martyrdom is the normal condition of the professed Christian."[4] So when the Gestapo finally breaks the door down to haul you away for confessing to Christ, it will be the merest externalization "of the inner reality out of which" you are, God help you, already living your life. "The early Christian martyrs talked of death with a horrible happiness,"[5] Chesterton reports. Setting their hearts on One finally transcendent to themselves, they went cheerfully to their deaths, in order that the memory of Him might live. No wonder, Chesterton says, "they smelt the grave afar off like a field of flowers."[6] Indeed, they had no doubt but that at the supreme moment of testing, Christ would reveal Himself as the One Who had come to vanquish death itself. For this reason, they remained fearless in the face of a pagan civilization hell-bent on their annihilation, a fearlessness, we now know, sublimely instrumental in bringing down that corrupt pagan world, substituting a Christian order whose flowering would survive a thousand years and more.

As a wickedly cynical Jesuit I used to know would often say, "You know, it's going to get worse before it gets a lot

---

[4] Rev. Hans Urs von Balthasar, *The Moment of Christian Witness* (Glen Rock, N.J.: Newman Press, 1969), 10.
[5] G. K. Chesterton, *Orthodoxy* (New York: Dodd, Mead and Company, 1946), 134.
[6] *Orthodoxy*, 134.

worse." So pray always for the grace of the present moment. Of course, the art of knowing how to waste time prodigiously with God, of resting simply in Him, is not as easily won as reading books about it while comfortably seated in an armchair sipping diet cola. It is a far easier thing, Tolstoy tells us somewhere, to produce twenty volumes of philosophy than to practice to perfection one of the Beatitudes. Count Leo, I suspect, had most definitely an easier time of it working up *War and Peace* than working out his own marriage (alas, the record shows he treated poor Mrs. Tolstoy rather shabbily). My first book, *The Suffering of Love: Christ's Descent into the Hell of Human Hopelessness*,[7] the fruit of a dissertation painstakingly produced in Rome some years back, was a whole lot easier to pull off than attempting to raise even one of my children. The intractibilities of dealing with kids, even the seraphic specimens I've got, easily exceed whatever challenges I may have faced in trying to fill blank sheets of paper. Talk about descents into hell! Why, in the time it has taken me to type only this page, there have been three hair-raising interruptions from the Lilliputians I live with, such that, had Mr. Swift only put them into the story, they would greatly have improved *Gulliver's Travels*—still leaving me, of course, "with the intolerable wrestle [w]ith words and meanings,"[8] to recall Eliot's lapidary line.

Then, of course, there are the importunities of students. How often I have been accosted by the freshly repentant undergraduate, who, following a prolonged moral holiday, will suddenly evince the most painful dismay at the fact that in becoming an earnest and upright citizen of the Kingdom,

---

[7] Petersham, Mass.: St. Bede's Publications, 1995.
[8] T. S. Eliot, *Four Quartets*, in *The Complete Poems and Plays: 1909-1950* (New York: Harcourt, Brace & World, 1971), 119.

he may yet require more than a weekend's retreat. ("Do you really mean to tell me, Doctor Martin, that I might not be ready for the grace of transforming union?")

What I'm saying, I guess, is this: that to find the "still point" of the turning world, "the point of intersection of the timeless / with time," will require a certain amount of time—great draughts of it, I'm afraid. But isn't that really rather comforting to know? What else is time but the medium through which we move from here to Heaven? Is there any other form of union with God apart from time, apart from Christ, whose own daring and headlong descent into that swirling mass, that unceasing surge, was expressly intended for our salvation? "Only through time," writes Eliot, "time is conquered."[9] So, yes, great heaping amounts will be needed from that river, each resolutely drawn in order to lay siege at the last to the truth and the meaning of our lives. But remember: it is grace that rides time like a river, or so Hopkins puts it in an inspired image.[10] Eliot says:

Men's curiosity searches past and future
And clings to that dimension. But to apprehend
The point of intersection of the timeless
With time, is an occupation for the saint—
No occupation either, but something given
And taken, in a lifetime's death in love,
Ardour and selflessness and self-surrender.[11]

---

[9] Eliot, *Four Quartets*, 120.
[10] Hopkins, "The Wreck of the Deutschland," in *The Poems of Gerard Manley Hopkins*, 53.
[11] Eliot, *Four Quartets*, 136.

All right, then, prayer (a kneeling theology,[12] Balthasar calls it) is in order. What else? Well, how about extending the courtesy we rightly owe God on over to those deputized by Him, in His Church, to teach theology—who, in professing it over years and years spent in fruitful study, may have learned a thing or two worth passing on? I always tell my students, half-jocularly, that if they really want to pick up the habit of thinking theologically, then they had better learn fast how to heed whatever I tell them. "Be intensely attentive to all that I say," I announce pompously on the first day. "A missed preposition may be permitted now and again, but surely not whole sentences. And very often even fragments are worth jotting down." And then, without a trace of flippancy, I let them know that what we're about here is an exceedingly important study, a discipline altogether indispensable to the maintenance of the university of which we happen to be members. "She's the blooming queen of all the sciences!" I fairly exult. "Don't you think, in the circumstance, we owe her a bit of deference?"

"So come to class," I tell them, "with all the constancy of pious nuns popping into the chapel to pray." I assure them, "Of course you needn't genuflect." (Even professors ought to keep their pretensions fairly modest.) "However," I add, "you'd jolly well better be on time. Otherwise," (I am fairly shouting at this point in the diatribe) "you risk gravely insulting your professor, which may be good for my humility,

---

[12] See Patriarch Angelo Scola's superb little study, *Hans Urs von Balthasar: A Theological Style* (Grand Rapids: Wm. B. Eerdmans, 1995), 4. "'Being on one's knees,'" he writes of Balthasar's style of doing theology, "'has nothing to do with demonstrations of piety intended to substitute for scholarly rigor . . . but rather with the posture of the theologian's heart, which is that of Paul on the road to Damascus: seized by the form of the glory and thrown to his knees in adoration.'"

but can hardly help your grade." That generally puts the fear of God into all but the most impenitent, that is, those whom I don't much care to teach anyway.

So this second presumption is really about the courtesy we owe the teacher who, if he has been faithful to his mistress, has already forgone great heaps of comfort and cash in order to mediate to his students something of the mysteries of God, which Mother Church holds in her heart for all the faithful to know. "He can no longer have God for his Father," warns Saint Cyprian of Carthage, "who has not the Church for his Mother."[13] One of the finest courses I had at the Angelicum, where I spent close to five wonderfully delightful years, was taught by a fussy old English Dominican, who once threatened an impertinent student with a tomato: "And if you persist, young man, in this practice, I shall commence throwing vegetables at you!" Oh my, how that man could bellow. I am sure the wrath of that moment had not been equaled in forty years, not since the great Garrigou-Lagrange held forth in stentorian Latin, back when a young Polish curate named Karol Wojtyla came to study. I hadn't the kidney, of course, to tell the eminent Father-professor, but inasmuch as tomatoes are really a kind of fruit, he oughtn't to have said vegetables. Still, he had a point (indeed, it nearly splattered across the pate of his student), which goes to the heart of the courtesy we owe to one who, as Dante said of Aristotle, is "the master of them that know."[14]

Ah, but it must never be an unearned expertise! Like cheap grace, it is instantly suspect in those who wear it too

---

[13] Saint Cyprian of Carthage, *On the Unity of the Church*, no. 6, as quoted at http://www.ccel.org/fathers2/ANF-05/anf05-111.htm.

[14] Dante Alighieri, canto IV, in *The Divine Comedy 1: Inferno* (New York: Oxford University Press, 1961), 65.

glibly. In what else, then, does this business of trusting the teacher consist? One useful way perhaps to think of it is in terms of the attorney-client relation. While the air may be filled with noise of litigation, amid all that horrific din, one fact nevertheless remains: the presumed innocence of the accused. It is what the lawyers like to call *tentative sympathy*, which I explain to my students this way: "Suppose," I tell them, "you have just been refused that financial aid package you'd been pining for, and rather than meekly submitting to this injustice, you proceed instead to hold at gunpoint the university vice president—until, that is, the money can safely be deposited in your account. Now listen carefully," I tell them, having just intimated a possible bloodbath in the financial aid office (no more hallowed precinct than which can be imagined), their rapt attention is ensured. "Notice that as farfetched as your alleged cries of innocence sound— I mean, the gun is literally about to go off!—it is precisely thanks to that presumption that your attorney is able to mount a credible defense."

Improbable, you say? Remember now, dear reader, we're dealing here with the first post-O.J. generation, not to mention our late unlamented president's troubles before a Congress nevertheless disposed to acquit so flagrant a miscreant. The patent credulity of the American people is something every successful politician can regularly depend on to keep his job.

But leave all that aside for a moment. What I have in mind here is not pejorative at all. Rather, it is a virtue, a very old fashioned one at that, called docility (not to be confused with servility), which implies an openness in terms of the student's willingness to be taught, to be filled with the Church's understanding of herself, her nature and finality. And, indeed, at the profoundest level, *all* the baptized are implicated already, insofar as having been baptized into her mysteries, it is their faith, too.

But as a practical matter, what specifically does docility mean? Well, to begin with, try a willing suspension of disbelief, misapprehension, fear, prejudice—whatever attitude or even conviction of hostility may be impeding the effort to reach them. The Church somehow has got to pierce the armor of all that prevents the world, and her own, from approaching Christ's Bride with that modicum of sympathy, which even the most hardened attorney extends to the poor fellow in the dock. The critic Mark Van Doren put it rather neatly when he wrote, "As every man is a philosopher of sorts, so every man is a theologian if he can see beyond his nose."[15]

Detachment of self, in other words, involving a certain discreet distancing of self, may be necessary in order really to see the Church. "Who knows," I tell my students, "maybe some of you back in the fourth grade were slapped by a sadistic nun?" (Certainly I was, repeatedly.) "And you have never gotten over the trauma, have you? Well, now is the time to try to put the experience behind you."

Can it be done? Good heavens, I hope so! After all, life is replete with examples of courtesies freely extended. Seeing the Church and the Persons of the Blessed Trinity is surely analogous to any number of imaginative leaps of sympathy we're routinely expected to make toward our wives, parents, roommates, or even characters in a novel. Do we not find ourselves suspending disbelief the moment we step into a movie theater? The houselights dim, the silver screen lights up, and an entire world unfolds, in the

---

[15] Mark Van Doren, *Liberal Education* (Boston: Beacon Press, 1959), 143.

essential unreality of which we willingly suspend our dis-belief. I remember watching *Tootsie* years ago, the lead character of which (was it Dustin Hoffman?) plays a woman and—great Scott!—I was quite persuaded by the success of the impersonation.

If an audience of jaded sophisticates can extend imaginative sympathy to an actor pretending to be a woman, is it any more of a stretch for that same audience to accommodate the persona of one who affects to speak truthfully about the Church? Who knows, if God is able to write straight with crooked lines, why can't a poor professor be the one holding the pencil?

CHAPTER III

THE COURTESY OWED OUR ANCESTORS

In any human endeavor, from Frisbee to fund-raising, the primary measure of success, it has been said, is intensity of attention, or, to put the thing less grandly, love. In order really to know someone or something, you have first got to love it. "Men did not love Rome because she was great," wrote Chesterton. "She was great because they had loved her."[1]

To go out of oneself, as it were, taking blessed leave of all that prevents or impedes that sheer *ex-stasis* (standing outside) of self—that is the key. Nothing less than ardent surrender to the thing you wish to know will do the trick. Take a risk before the otherness of it, and—bingo!—the butterfly (or other object of knowledge) is yours. Only then will it yield up its secret, giving you occasion to rejoice.

So the wise teacher will tell his students that they must become vulnerable to whatever truths Christ wishes to impart to them—yes, even if they must find mediation through me, this poor player who struts his hour upon the stage of your mind, and, four months later, is heard no more.

Here is a copybook example of what I have in mind. Take the licentious moralist who pronounces virtue better than vice. Now even though you and I might imagine it all quite differently (aided, who can doubt, by the immoralities of

---

[1] G. K. Chesterton, *Orthodoxy* (New York: Dodd, Mead and Company, 1946), 123.

the moralist), nevertheless we have really got to try to countenance the unthinkable possibility that he may be right. Or, again, that bank we imagine divesting a couple thousand dollars of, or the answer we'd dearly love to pilfer from a neighbor's exam—such swindles, we must tell ourselves, are really not going to make us happy or complete human beings. Despite the insidious twist of desire that turns it all to seeming delight, there can never be any percentage in making perverse choices. And the truth of the proposition does not in the least depend on the integrity of the person making it. Is Christ less present in the Eucharist because the priest who confected it happens to be a frequent sinner? No—not any more than that the sum of two plus two is a function of the arithmetician's moral standing in the community.

Thus, by the same logic, when Christ's Bride disports herself as holy and immaculate, the skeptic must not all at once rush to judgment about strumpets and whores polluting the Kingdom of Heaven. The Church, to recall the Pauline teaching, "*is* his body, the fulness of him who fills all in all" (Eph. 1:23, emphasis added). Does she cease to be God's Body because of this or that defiled member? We must remember this: Our God is an ironical God, Who can effortlessly make straight even the most colossally crooked lines. Think it possible, then, that the frowzy and fallen woman dancing like a drunken dervish before the tabernacle of the living God is in actual fact wedded to the very One before Whose altar she worships. What else can it mean to call the Church His Bride?

Now having ended the last chapter on a somewhat crooked note, suppose we continue along that same line to see whether, as the proverb would have us believe, God really is free to write straight with it. To that end, I propose the following story, which, so help me, will cast a most piercing light on this whole matter of Mother Church and the sympathy which, if only tentatively, she is entitled to receive. Back when I was a student in college, I knew a fellow by the name of Eddie. Bizarre in every way, he was often seen flitting about the campus like an antic bird. Oh, he was a geeky guy! By the end of the first week of his freshman year, he'd not only bought every book he expected to read in four years of university education but also, incredibly, managed to join every available club, fraternity, and athletic team on campus as well. (Alas, poor Eddie, he could not then know that by early December he'd be a dropout, his world having come completely unglued. But that's another story.)

Anyway, Eddie and I lived on the same floor as freshmen, which often threw us into one another's company, and early on in the acquaintance, he started telling me all about his girlfriend and her countless and exquisite graces and accomplishments, of which I soon wearied of hearing. It was a line that seemed to me at the time about as completely crooked as anything I had ever heard. Finally, in exasperation, I fairly exploded, forbidding him ever to speak of her again. "Spare me the details of your fraudulent dream goddess," I remember saying with some heat. "Let me see this fabled apparition of yours, and I'll judge for myself." (Even then, you see, the wheels of revenge were beginning to turn in my mind, intending to run over poor Eddie. "If she's this gorgeous," I thought to myself, "and he's such a nerd, perhaps I'll steal her away?")

So the long-awaited apparition finally revealed itself, and, well, she was really quite spectacularly unattractive— the most perfectly, boringly plain Jane I'd ever seen. What was he thinking? How could he not know? And then it hit me: He loved her! She was lovely because he loved her. Of course, she was lovely, God having first loved her into existence; even the dullest looking among us will give off glints of His glory. It was only by the sheerest blind folly on my part that I failed to see the fact. But young Eddie possessed the eye of a lover, looking with perpetual longing at his lady. He took this frowzy thing and saw her framed with the light of heaven. She bore the very weight of glory to him. And, after all, is not his view confirmed by the fact of Christology itself? "For Christ plays in ten thousand places," to quote Hopkins' superb lyric, "Lovely in limbs, and lovely in eyes not his / To the Father through the features of men's faces."[2]

She *was* lovely in his eyes, you see, because by his love he had transmuted her into loveliness. "Who speaks the things that love him shows," writes Coventry Patmore, "shall say things deeper than he knows."[3] Eddie knew. This bird-like fellow, whom I'd been tempted falsely to dismiss as a mere besotted chump, was besotted all right, but not by anything false. An experience of true beauty had so ravished his heart, so entirely turned his head, that he might never be the same again. As a result of that transforming encounter with Eros—the beatrician moment of his young life—Eddie had begun his promised ascent to such joy and beauty as might someday usher him into the precincts of eternal felicity. "A kind of dreadful perfection," writes Charles Williams of this first blessed encounter of Dante with Beatrice, "has appeared in the streets of Florence;

---

[2] Rev. Gerard Manley Hopkins, S.J., "'As kingfishers catch fire, dragonflies draw flame,'" in *The Poems of Gerard Manley Hopkins*, 4th ed. (London: Oxford University Press, 1967), 90.

[3] Coventry Patmore, "Fragments," in *The Poems of Coventry Patmore*, ed. Frederick Page (London: Oxford University Press, 1949), 479.

something like the glory of God walking down the street towards him."[4]

Yes, Rome is great because men have surely loved her. And no love is greater than that lavished upon the Church by Christ Himself, Whose Holy Spirit animates her life at every turn, rendering her inexpressibly lovely.

And for how very long a time, too! Here I touch on the third and final presumption for seeing the splendor of Christ's Church: namely, the sense of tradition, or history, or the past, which remains altogether intrinsic to her. Old Mother Church has been around practically forever. In fact, a look at the second vision of the Shepherd of Hermas, written sometime in the second century, will indicate just how long. He beholds in his mind's eye an image of an aged woman, whom he mistakenly thinks might be the Sibyl. But it is not she. "Who then is she?" he asks. "The Church." "Wherefore then is she aged?" he then asks. "Because . . . she was created before all things; therefore is she aged; and for her sake the world was framed."[5]

What an absolutely astonishing assertion! She, the Church, was instituted not because of man's sin, but because of God's splendor. And He, God, thought of His Bride, this beloved Body, from all eternity as a way of bringing to perfection, of carrying to a most sublime pitch of perfection, the Glory of the Lord, Jesus Christ. God's Word is wedded thus to the world through this woman, the Bride, Mother Church.

---

[4] Charles Williams, *The Figure of Beatrice: A Study in Dante* (n.p.: Noonday, 1961; reprint, New York: Octagon Books, 1983), 20.
[5] The Shepherd of Hermas, *Vision 2*, no. 4[8]:1, as quoted at http://www.early christianwritings.com/text/shepherd-lightfoot.html.

In this circumstance, it is vitally important to try and get students to see the timelessness of the Church into whose saving waters they were once baptized. Heaven knows, their own horizons, so often circumscribed by the here and now, seldom venture beyond the events of the immediate past: the undercooked lasagna at lunch, yesterday's unread letter, the assignment unfinished from last week. "He who is ignorant of what happened before his birth," warned Cicero, "is always a child."[6] How many of the students of today's world remain trapped in childhood!

There are a couple of ways, however, to try to awaken them, to stir the pot of that sweet solipsism which is youth. One way is simply to ask at the beginning of term how many persons are present. "All right, give me an inventory of all the persons here today," I announce. And after they fumble about a bit with the numbers (forty or so, say), I then take exaggerated pleasure in swatting down the figure. "Surely there are more than that?" I'll say with mock disbelief. "What about your guardian angels, have you included them? Don't they possess souls? Aren't they persons? They think and will, don't they?" And, yes, the sheer doubling of the number (or higher, given the fact that some students, the intransigent ones, can probably boast of several hovering angels), does contribute to a certain enrichment of the sensibility. For if, as Chesterton avers, "it ought to be the oldest things that are taught to the youngest people,"[7] then it would surely be impoverishing not to include news about creatures much older than ourselves, indeed, such separated

---

[6] Cicero, quoted in Mark Van Doren, *Liberal Education* (Boston: Beacon Press, 1959), 118.

[7] G. K. Chesterton, *What's Wrong with the World?* (New York: Dodd, Mead and Company, 1910), 255.

substances (so Aquinas called them) who exist in order to praise God and help us all to Heaven.[8]

The other example is perhaps more pointed, and turning on a very old tradition far back in the Church's past, may jolt the student with a sudden and surprising shock into an awareness of how fleeting one's brief moment in history actually is. That is the matter of levels or states of membership in Christ's Mystical Body. "If very nearly all the Catholics who ever lived are already dead," I announce portentously, "where does that leave thee and me?" The silence, while perhaps not stunned, is certainly palpable. Dead? This bears a bit of pondering, to be sure. But, yes, it is true: If Catholicism consists of a succession of members moving in pilgrim fashion from life to death—from Church militant on earth, to Church suffering in purgatory, to (please God!) Church triumphant in heaven—then undeniably most of the baptized have already gone home to God.

All of this implies, does it not, that a certain grace of humility ought to inform the movements and deliberations of those who, in Chesterton's immortal phrase, "merely happen to be walking about?" Here is the heart of the matter, it seems to me, and no one has given it more striking expression than Chesterton himself, whose masterful dissection of the "democracy of the dead" is just the antidote young people today need to overcome that idolatry with which so many of us adorn the present. He writes, "[T]radition is only democracy extended through time. . . . Tradition means giving votes to the most obscure of all classes, our ancestors. It is the democracy of the dead. Tradition refuses to submit

---

[8] Saint Thomas Aquinas, *Summa Theologica*, I, q. 54, art. 5.

to the small and arrogant oligarchy of those who merely happen to be walking about."[9]

Isn't that glorious? Ah, but there is more to come. Chesterton goes on to note how, just as no democrat would dream of depriving a man of his right to vote because of the accident of birth, so too the traditionalist is loath to disenfranchise someone on account of the accident of death. In short, we owe even the dead the courtesy of extending deference to them; the ancestral counsels must be taken if we are not to break faith with those who have gone before us. This sense of the past, which includes a lively awareness of the diaphanous frontiers we move across from time present to time past, and myriad ancestral collisions along the way, is not something any one of us can easily acquire. Indeed, it is not like family possessions automatically passed on from one generation to another. If we desire this patrimony at all, we must obtain it at great cost. As T. S. Eliot writes in a seminal essay called "Tradition and the Individual Talent" (from a book of essays called *The Sacred Wood* written around 1920, which fairly launched his reputation as the finest critic of his generation): "[T]he historical sense involves a perception, not only of the pastness of the past, but of its presence. . . . This historical sense, which is a sense of the timeless as well as of the temporal and of the timeless and of the temporal together, is what makes a writer traditional. And it is at the same time what makes a writer most acutely conscious of his place in time, of his own contemporaneity."[10]

---

[9] Chesterton, *Orthodoxy*, 84-85.
[10] T. S. Eliot, *The Sacred Wood* (London: Methuen & Co., 1964), 49.

Now Eliot is not writing theology here, but the point surely applies to the task of the theologian; for what else is faith seeking understanding, if not a total confrontation with the past, whose resources may then be used to repristinate the present? A whole movement of theology, in fact, bent on returning to the sources—back to bedrock!—has sought to root its understanding precisely in that sort of project: an intensive effort at recovering the past, distilling from its record an enduring substance.

In other words, this historical sense (recalling Eliot) permits a man to think and feel not simply as a member of this present generation (which, like all things mortal, will shortly pass away, scattering like the snows of yesteryear), but to fill one's mind and heart with all the generations that have gone before, stretching all the way back to that first generation of Adam and Eve and their countless progeny, at the very dawn of human history. All that history, says Eliot, must somehow become of a piece with this present moment. "[T]he difference between the present and the past," he writes, "is that the conscious present is an awareness of the past in a way and to an extent which the past's awareness of itself cannot show."[11]

I become conscious of my children's past, their tapestry of days gone by, in ways that they are simply not capable of knowing. When I see my daughters Francesca and Margaret, for example, perched precariously on the edge of maidenhood, I have a kind of double vision: They look more and more like their lovely mother, yet, at the same time, remain the little girls they used to be. Or, to take a secular example, we Americans, who know men like Washington and

---

[11] Eliot, *The Sacred Wood*, 52.

Jefferson and Lincoln, know them in ways they could never have known themselves, or know that republic they had so decisive a hand in shaping, simply by knowing them, knowing the ambient shape of their lives. First, we know them in the context of their own time, with its peculiarities of circumstance, but combined, too, with that cumulative collision with our own time, without which the circle of understanding is incomplete. When the young man confronted Eliot with the news that the dead writers were remote from us, that we know so much more than they did, he was bluntly told yes, and they are that which we know. We only know the dead masters. And were we to break faith with that wisdom on whose ample shoulders we stand (which is why we stand so tall or see so far), we would at once end in a ditch of bloody ignorance. Only the past exists; it alone is real.

How infinitely more telling Eliot's point appears when it is Christ Himself on Whose shoulders we stand—and the Church's, which He founded and which, on Christ's own authority, aims to prolong that strength of supernatural presence and power in time. Only surrender to that fact, I tell my students, which infinitely transcends our own paltry points in time, and—presto!—you find yourself enriched and extended in the most breath-catching ways, swept utterly out of and beyond yourselves into that sacred space which is God. You will know at last that *there* is the grace-filled finality man was made for, the life he presently longs for.

CHAPTER IV

WHILE
ANGELO SLEPT

The story is sometimes told of Blessed John XXIII that late at night, when feeling fretful about the state of the Church, he would at once ask himself, "Angelo? Who's running the Church, Angelo or the Holy Spirit? All right, then, go to bed."[1]

In short, good Pope John was possessed of an impregnably serene soul. "We are here on earth not to guard a museum," he would say, "but to cultivate a garden flourishing with life and promised to a glorious future."[2] Christ did not come to build the museum whose walls we stand watch outside of, but to give us life, His life, which He intended for our divinization. The Church and her members are thus loved and upheld by God unconditionally, their acceptance the result not of human or institutional merit but of grace, the sheer irrevocability of which renders us holy and blameless in His sight.

And so old Angelo slept undisturbed by the storms that swirled about outside, storms that, like wolves in search of sheep, threatened those little ones over whom God had appointed him their Shepherd. Likewise, too, for all the faithful of holy Church, the matter of her ultimate governance must never be in the least doubt either. Not to think as Angelo Roncalli did, and thereupon serenely to sleep, is

---

[1] Cf. *Wit and Wisdom of Good Pope John*, collected by Henri Fesquet, trans. Salvator Attanasio (New York: P. J. Kenedy and Sons, 1964), 45.
[2] *Wit and Wisdom of Good Pope John*, 161.

to court disaster; worse, it is to surrender the very citadel against which has been promised—by God Himself!—that not even the gates of hell would prevail.

But a funny thing happened on the way home from Vatican II. In the confused and chaotic aftermath of the council, word got around that the unthinkable had happened: While the pope and all his faithful slept, old Mother Church had up and married the spirit of the age, leaving her children bereft and, soon thereafter, herself a widow.

Do you think that an exaggeratedly bleak picture of apostasy and ruin? A scenario of disaster perhaps to which only pessimists are drawn—pessimists of a darkly reactionary hue? Maybe so. Nevertheless, the true picture was certainly troubling enough to move Blessed John's successor, Pope John Paul II, to convoke, in 1985 (twenty years after the council), an extraordinary synod precisely in order to call the Church to order, back to bedrock, back to those transcendent roots that bind her to God, roots that she was in some peril of forgetting. (Or rather we, the members of holy Church, were more and more inclined to forget.)

Indeed, the exact proportions of the crisis were such that the pope's right-hand man, the redoubtable Joseph Cardinal Ratzinger, prefect of the Congregation for the Doctrine of the Faith, was similarly moved that same year to unburden *his* soul, in an astonishingly frank series of interviews to an Italian journalist, Vittorio Messori, concerning the awful dangers that threaten a Church unmindful of her past, her memory, her point of origin. The result was *The Ratzinger Report*, which provoked a firestorm of controversy among Catholics the world over, including the usual suspects in this country, who savaged it from sea to shining sea.

How deliciously I recall those days. I was a student at the time, racing across Rome each morning in a crowded subway bound for the Angelicum, clutching my well-thumbed copy of *The Ratzinger Report*, which seemed to me revelatory of all that had gone wrong in the heady days after the council. What a splendid exposé of chuckleheaded theology he brought off in those few pages! It seemed to me the very quintessence of sanity at a time when not a few churchmen had gone quite off their heads. Small wonder that they sought in every quarter to revile him, tarring him with the brush even of fascism. The panzer prefect strikes again. The humor of it was only a bit less limp than the logic. I fell out of my subway seat watching him skewer all the talking heads of revisionist theology.

"Developments since the Council seem to be in striking contrast to the expectations of all," he noted. "What the Popes and the Council Fathers were expecting was a new Catholic unity, and instead one has encountered a dissension which—to use the words of Paul VI—seems to have passed over from self-criticism to self-destruction."[3] That was the flavor of the thing, all right.

The cardinal spoke wistfully of a new springtime, of vaunted hopes set in motion by the conciliar experience itself. Alas, he conceded, the expectation of all that exultant rhetoric ended abruptly in boredom and ennui. The Church thereupon found herself confronted, not by fresh reforms, but an enveloping decadence, and an eructation of disease and disorder "that to a large measure has been unfolding under the sign of a summons to a presumed 'spirit of the Council' and by so doing has actually and increasingly discredited it."[4]

---

[3] Joseph Cardinal Ratzinger with Vittorio Messori, *The Ratzinger Report* (San Francisco: Ignatius Press, 1985), 29.

[4] *The Ratzinger Report*, 30.

Scrubbed down, the problem is ecclesiology, that is, the Church's understanding of herself. While evidence of disintegration may be found anywhere—from depleted pews, rectories, and religious houses, with not a few survivors in a state either of shell shock or mutiny, to aberrations of liturgy, catechetics, and morality—what remains at the heart of the Church's crisis is the failure to understand who she is and what work God has given her to do. A felt loss of identity and mission seems to have bedeviled the Church at every turn—all this, moreover, at the very moment when ecclesial self-understanding, self-confidence, sublimely expressed in the council's document on the Church, had achieved maximum expression. If the twentieth century is the age of the Church, inaugurating a period of profound self-examination, then the fruits of such intense, protracted reflection can be found in the conciliar experience itself, most particularly its high-water mark, the Dogmatic Constitution on the Church, that is, *Lumen Gentium*, which throws a piercing light on the whole mystery of the Church. But as the redoubtable Doctor Johnson once said of a novel written by William Congreve, "I would rather praise it than read it."[5]

O sweetest of ironies! It was as if the more one learned of one's own mother, the less disposed one felt to love her. Such bizarre imbalance between the aim of the council and its aftermath cries out for analysis. All those sugarplums suddenly turned to dust and ashes; what had gone wrong? From a promised new Pentecost to Babylonian Captivity—how

---

[5] Samuel Johnson, quoted in W. Jackson Bate, *Samuel Johnson* (New York: Harcourt Brace Jovanovich, 1975), 535. Actually, the novel in question was an early effort so perhaps over time the muse improved the quality of his work and, by extension, Johnson's assessment.

could so much disillusion have set in so soon? Is it possible that in fact many in the Church had simply misunderstood the central intuition of the text, enshrined in the title itself, which points not to the Church, but to Christ: that He is the true *Lumen gentium*, or light of nations, of which she, the Church, remains at best the reflection? Could that have been the problem: the failure to see that while the document may be about her, the title rather gives it all to Him? Only permit the paradox and—bingo!—all details of Church doctrine and life fall effortlessly into place. Miss it and, well, a miasma of disaffection and distrust is spread abroad to infect the Body of Christ.

Certainly to an alarming and—who knows?—even unprecedented extent, opinion since the council has hardened around various reductionist models of the Church, her nature, and her purpose; the tendency of each has been to view her as so many disposable parts harnessed to ends entirely set by men. But is the Church really only externality, a thing to be manipulated as one might manipulate any other institution shaped by history? "Many no longer believe that what is at issue is a reality willed by the Lord himself," reports Cardinal Ratzinger. "Even with some theologians, the Church appears to be a human construction, an instrument created by us and one which we ourselves can freely reorganize according to the requirements of the moment."[6]

Such dangerous nonsense. Certainly the Church's membership consists of fallen human beings (why else was she instituted if not to help redeem them?), at liberty more or less to reshape her external visage. "But behind this,"

---

[6] *The Ratzinger Report*, 45.

warns the prefect, "the fundamental structures are willed by God himself, and therefore they are inviolable. Behind the *human* exterior stands the mystery of a *more than human* reality, in which reformers, sociologists, organizers have no authority whatsoever."[7]

In fact, at the deepest level, the Church, like her analogue, the moon, radiates a light belonging wholly to Another, to Christ. One does not draw near to an institution whose structures magically emit light and life; one draws near to a Person, to Christ, Whom the structures are meant to mediate. The sympathy or warmth I feel towards my neighbor in the pew we share does not compel my assent, but rather the salvation offered to him and me through those very mediating structures we call the Church. I am committed to the Church, therefore, because she exists in virtue of Him, because Christ graciously joined Himself to her, and because I am unlikely ever to find my way home to Him apart from her. But it is not she, not the moon, whose light I see, but the light of Christ, which she exists to impart in the medium of this world.

"The essence of the Church," Cardinal Ratzinger wrote many years ago in a passage worthy of Saint John of the Cross, "is that it counts for nothing in itself, in that the thing about it that counts is what it is not, in that it exists only to be dispossessed, in that it possesses a light that it is not and because of which alone it nonetheless is."[8] And thus, as he would later insist before the synod, it is of utmost

---

[7] *The Ratzinger Report*, 46.
[8] Joseph Cardinal Ratzinger, *Being Christian*, in *Two Say Why* (Chicago: Franciscan Herald Press, 1971), 79.

importance that the Church understand herself primarily as mystery (note: the very first chapter of *Lumen Gentium* is called "The Mystery of the Church"), as the sacrament of Someone transcendent to herself. "The division of power in the Church could not be the central theme of the Synod. Moreover a Church that speaks too much of herself, does not in truth speak well of herself."[9]

Of Whom she is meant to speak could not be more plain: The Church is charged with speaking the Word of One Who remains the perpetual font of her being, her fruitfulness. Here, by the way, is the thread running through all the documents of Vatican II, which the pope's synod took considerable pains to retrace. The trouble is, of course, scarcely anyone these days is terribly interested. Certainly in the case of the progressive wing, the whole conciliar event has ceased to matter very much. It was at best a prelude to much greater things to come, a launching pad, as it were, for more radical reforms that, according to Cardinal Ratzinger, have led to "the unleashing *within* the Church of latent polemical and centrifugal forces."[10] These forces, in combination with the Church's "confrontation with a cultural revolution in the West,"[11] have nearly succeeded in wrecking the enterprise altogether.

We have simply got to get back to bedrock, back to the source of that self-understanding ratified by the Church herself, whose supreme confession of faith places her profoundly and inescapably in relation to Christ. Let Christ's

---

[9] Joseph Cardinal Razinger, Intervention at the Extraordinary Assembly of the Synod of Bishops of 1985, in "Fourth General Congregation," *L'Osservatore Romano*, 9 December 1985, p. 6.
[10] *The Ratzinger Report*, 30.
[11] *The Ratzinger Report*, 30.

light, the blessed radiation from which fills the world with His Person, pierce the darkness that surrounds us.

The time is long overdue for us Roman Catholics, beneficiaries after all of the council, to reacquaint ourselves with the Church as mystery, which is the deepest point of entry into her life, her fruitfulness. *Lumen Gentium* shows us the way. Let us return, then, to the source, to the text of whose meaning we can never come to an end.

CHAPTER V

MISTAKING GOD FOR GOLF

Some years ago, on a train bound for Boston, I found myself seated across from two women, a mother and her daughter, the latter possessing an enormous vanity case into whose depths she would regularly disappear for what seemed like hours of cosmetic reconstruction. Between makeovers, she would hit me with hard questions. "So what do you *do*?" she'd ask. I told her that I taught theology. "What's that?" she demanded. When I said to her that it was the study of God, she looked somewhat puzzled, but said nothing. Soon thereafter, she went back to the vanity case. Nothing more was said until we pulled into South Station and I rose to go. "Where," she suddenly blurted out, "are your golf clubs?" Incredulous that anyone should think I'd be carrying sports equipment on a train to Boston, I asked what on earth possessed her to say that. Besides, I added, I detest golf. "Didn't you say you were a theologian?" she protested. "Well, isn't that the study of *golf*?"

It was moment of utter, supreme hilarity, the irony of which I savored all the way to Lancaster, Massachusetts, where, thanks to a kind Providence, my future bride awaited me, though neither of us knew it at the time. (But that's another story.) Meanwhile, the encounter with the confused young girl who mistook God for golf is an endlessly instructive one. It leads very nicely, I think, to the point of this chapter.

Theology is really about God. The very word *theology*, in fact, means study or truth (*logos*) about God (*Theos*). Thus He remains the central figure, the main character as it were in the story, all the rest being fairly peripheral to His own dazzling performance. Theology is a sacred science, therefore, not reducible to our potty little selves, but gloriously, recalcitrantly transcendent to everything, even as it casts the most piercing light upon everything else. There is neither nature nor artifice to surpass the being of God. The study of Him ought, therefore, to antedate anything else; it will surely include everything else since God not only possesses His own being but holds the world and ourselves in being as well.

And never mind the anthropocentric conceits of crackpot theologians, who turn God into a kind of twelve-step program for improving the world. For instance, the late William Sloan Coffin, Jr., chaplain to a generation of students at Yale, often described faith as a sort of floating craps game, concerning which the only relevant question to ask is, Where's the action today?

Horsefeathers. God is the action, and He remains eternally, effortlessly present to Himself. "The more you know God," writes the angelic pilgrim Angelus Silesius, "the more you will confess that what He is Himself, you can name less and less."[1] Even His initiative to save us from our own sinful folly altogether precedes whatever endeavor we might mount. Whatever be the sequence in which things are set, God is always in advance of our arriving at it. He

---

[1] *Angelus Silesius: The Cherubinic Wanderer*, trans. Maria Shrady (New York: Paulist Press, 1986), x.

has gone before us on life's road in order to accompany us from the start, and when we reach the end, He will have been there already. If the axiom from Aquinas be true that "all knowers know God implicitly in all they know,"[2] nevertheless the God Whom they know remains always more than what they know. For the fruit of such knowledge, as in the myth of Tantalus, is finally beyond the reach of human understanding.

So God does not need thee or me, or the world for that matter, to prove His mettle. His perfections are not dependent upon the mess we've made of things, which, by somehow entering the universe to be solved, helps shore up His own importance. A God Whose importance depended on the work given Him to do by the world is not a definition of God, but of government—hardly the stuff of salvation, I'm afraid.

This accounts for why, from the fourth century onward, the Church Fathers carefully distinguished between *Who* God is in Himself, that is, the eternal processions of Father, Son, and Holy Spirit, and *what* God has undertaken to do on our behalf, that is, the temporal missions of Creator, Redeemer, and Sanctifier. The approach, therefore, to the meaning of God's being-in-Himself, that is, the immanent Trinitarian life of God—the inner landscape, as it were, of God Himself—was what doing theology fundamentally meant. On the other hand, the approach to the meaning of all that He has done for us, namely, the complete emptying of His life into the life of man—the external relations giving shape to the whole history of salvation—was not properly theology at all but rather economy (*dispensatio* in

---

[2] Saint Thomas Aquinas, *De veritate*, q. XXII, art. 2, ad 1.

the Latin), which included God's work of rescuing the world from total ruin.

Of course, we only come to an understanding of the processions within the Godhead as a result of the missions without; what God does becomes more or less revelatory of Who God is. Confronted with the sheer scale of God's salvific work in the world, in which the heart of God is pierced by a world whose wickedness He has come to redeem, the mind is suddenly vouchsafed the great discovery, for there at the edge of eternity itself one peers into an abyss of absolute, unfathomable divine love. Like Dante's geometer in the final canto of the *Paradiso*, who sets himself to square the circle, yet cannot divine the formula he needs to unpuzzle the problem, the mind reels before the mystery of "how the image was fitted to the circle and how it has its place there."[3] How, in other words, to reconcile the two realities: the direct vision of the eternal, unchanging God, and the human face worn by the Incarnate Word, Whom Dante, positively stunned by the realization, sees at its center? He confesses: "[B]ut my own wings were not sufficient for that, had not my mind been smitten by a flash wherein came its wish. Here power failed the high phantasy; but now my desire and will, like a wheel that spins with even motion, were revolved by the Love that moves the sun and the other stars."[4]

So profound an abyss is this depth of God, the always greater God, that one can never come to an end of it. Only the Word may speak with perfect adequacy of Who and what God is. And are we better than He, that our speech could possibly encompass the range and reality of One Who

---

[3] Dante Alighieri, canto XXXIII, in *The Divine Comedy 3: Paradiso*, trans. John D. Sinclair (New York: Oxford University Press, 1961), 485.
[4] *The Divine Comedy 3: Paradiso*, 485.

must remain finally unnameable? "If all things were within our grasp," says Saint Gregory of Nyssa, "the higher Power would not be beyond us."[5] It is the mysterious note of apophysis, of negation and denial, on which all talk of God is finally struck, lest the busy scrutiny of little minds (when it comes to God all minds are little) disrupt the mystery of God's sheer Otherness.

Yet God does truly show Himself in His Word made flesh; He does not altogether withdraw the blessed efficacy of His being behind a cloud of complete unknowing. God shows us the "in Himself" side of His mystery amid the equally incomprehensible mystery of being "for us," the famous *pro nobis* of all the many confessional paradigms of Catholic Christendom, creedal forms on which our dignity and salvation depend. (How endearing the Chestertonian formulation, namely that to take away the Nicene Creed is to "do some strange wrong to the seller of sausages"!)[6] As Henri de Lubac observes, citing the text of the Common Doctor, Saint Thomas Aquinas, "We glimpse the '*occultum divinitatis*' [hiddenness of divinity] only through the '*mysterium humanitatis*' [mystery of Christ's humanity], in whom the entire economy resides—and is transcended."[7]

But, once again, we must not reduce the one to the other, with the result that God collapses into sheer functionality, as if He had nothing better to do for all eternity except think

---

[5] The quote appears on the front piece setting off a superb study of the religious thought of Gregory of Nyssa by Hans Urs von Balthasar: *Presence and Thought: Essay on the Religious Philosophy of Gregory of Nyssa*, trans. Mark Sebanc (San Francisco: Ignatius Press, 1988), 7.

[6] G. K. Chesterton, *Heretics* (New York: John Luce Co., 1905), 99.

[7] Henri Cardinal de Lubac, S.J., *The Christian Faith: An Essay on the Structure of the Apostle's Creed*, trans. Brother Richard Arnandez, F.S.C. (San Francisco: Ignatius Press, 1986), 91.

happy thoughts about us. Yes, God is in the details, but no, He is not one of the details. You and I remain, therefore, not only recipients of a salvation we could never ourselves give, but one the nature of which primarily derives from the being of a God Who eternally is, before reaching us (secondarily) by virtue of what this same God historically does. In this, we are to see the complete primacy of being over doing, logos over ethos, theology over economy.

Is this not immediately borne out by the structure of all the ancient creeds of the Church, beginning with the apostles? On what foundational truth do the momentous assertions of apostolic belief depend, if not on God? "I believe in God, the Father almighty..." What else does belief begin with if not a God Who is without beginning? And where does it all end, if not eternal life for men with the God Who, finally, is without end? And between the two eternities of God, what exactly have we got? Only one thing, and that is time, time whose rhythms God in Christ perfectly passed through, and which faith requires that we, too, enter and move through as pilgrims on our homeward journey. How beautiful the words of Pope John Paul II, introducing the great theme of millennial jubilee: "The whole of the Christian life is like a great *pilgrimage to the house of the Father*, whose unconditional love for every human creature, and in particular for the 'prodigal son' (cf. Lk. 15:11-32), we discover anew each day."[8]

This basic truth may also be illustrated by reference to the *Catechism*, which reads: "God, infinitely perfect and blessed in himself, in a plan of sheer goodness freely created man to

---

[8] Pope John Paul II, Apostolic Letter on Preparation for the Jubilee of the Year 2000 *Tertio Millennio Adveniente* (November 10, 1994), no. 49, emphasis in original.

make him share in his own blessed life. For this reason, at every time and in every place, God draws close to man. He calls man to seek him, to know him, to love him with all his strength. He calls together all men, scattered and divided by sin, into the unity of his family, the Church" (no. 1).

God does not create a world—nor people it with beings formed from His own image—out of grim necessity. There are no constraints in God requiring that He do this or that, no iron laws of contingency to hamstring or limit in any way the operation of the sovereign Lord of the universe. He creates out of delight, the pure pleasure of making beings be. Indeed, if Chesterton is to be believed, God is such that He exults even in monotony. Is it not possible, he asks, that every morning, God says to the sun, "Do it again!" and then at day's end He will say the same to the moon? "It may not be automatic necessity that makes all daisies alike; it may be that God makes every daisy separately, but has never got tired of making them . . . that He has the eternal appetite of infancy; for we have sinned and grown old, and our Father is younger than we."[9] "We are such stuff as dreams are made on,"[10] Shakespeare tells us. And the saints, do they not all exclaim that we are the amazement of God?

Or take this splendid opening from *Lumen Gentium*, announcing the theme of the entire conciliar text: "Christ is the Light of nations."[11] What can this mean but that all salvation, all the happiness of heaven, comes by and

---

[9] G. K. Chesterton, *Orthodoxy* (New York: Dodd, Mead and Company, 1946), 108-9.

[10] William Shakespeare, *The Tempest*, in *Major Plays and the Sonnets* (New York: Harcourt, Brace and Company, 1948), act IV, sc. I, 1025.

[11] Second Vatican Council, Dogmatic Constitution on the Church *Lumen Gentium* (November 21, 1964), no. 1.

through Him? It is not any of us who can generate this light; we are not swashbuckling sources of anything save our own miserable sins. But by our relationship to Him, which takes place in that surpassing nuptial bond between Christ, the Head, and His Body, the Church (cf. Eph. 5:32), we enter into profound sacramental union with the living God Himself, as a result of which all creation may be brought home to God.

It is Christ alone, then, Who remains the Light of all the world. And, to be sure, He does not come to earth to conceal the light of which He alone is the source. No, He desires to share it, to diffuse such as He Himself is to the very ends of the earth. Not to see this is really to miss the point of the text, to miss as well the overarching aim of the council, which longs to midwife Christ to the world, "to bring the light of Christ to all men, a light brightly visible on the countenance of the Church."[12] After all, she, the Church, *is* in Christ in the form of a sacrament, "a sacrament or as a sign and instrument both of a very closely knit union with God and of the unity of the whole human race."[13]

Her mission, then, is very simply to bring Christ to the world. "[A]nd I, when I am lifted up from the earth, will draw all men to myself" (Jn. 12:32). Who else but the Church, which, in the words of the great Bossuet, is Jesus Christ "spread abroad and passed on,"[14] exists to raise up God before the world?

---

[12] *Lumen Gentium*, no. 1.

[13] *Lumen Gentium*, no. 1.

[14] Most Rev. Jacques-Benigne Bossuet, "Allucution aux Nouvelles Catholiques," in *Oeuvres Oratoires*, vol. iv (n.p., n.d.), 508, quoted in Henri Cardinal de Lubac, S.J., *The Splendor of the Church*, trans. Michael Mason (San Francisco: Ignatius Press, 1986), 48. Here is the passage wherein he quotes Bishop

Here is how the Venerable Newman has described the relationship between God and the Church:

> And I love supremely, solely,
> Him the holy, Him the strong.
> And I hold in veneration,
> For the love of Him alone,
> Holy Church, as His creation,
> And her teachings, as His own.[15]

The lines are from his poetic masterpiece "The Dream of Gerontius," which depicts the journey of a soul poised on the rim of death, anxious to return to God, yet determined at the last to get it absolutely right, so that, fortified by the grace of Christ's Cross, he may be spared an endless loss. What may we most firmly and truly believe, Newman asks, without which no life, however healthy or prosperous, is worth living? And, most urgent of all, where are we to find this living faith? For Newman, the answer could not have been more clear or more consoling. The best and most secure setting for all that faith holds out for us to discover and defend is holy Church herself, whom we are to love precisely because Christ died to bring her to life. "He can no longer have God for his Father," warns Saint Cyprian, "who has not the Church for his Mother,"[16] or indeed, the Church whose very Spirit, the Third Person of the Blessed Trinity,

---

Bossuet: "For, granted that the Church is really Christ perpetuated among us, Christ 'spread abroad and passed on', still the Church's members, lay and clerical, are not the inheritors of the privilege which caused Christ to say so boldly: 'Which of you shall convict me of sin?'" (Jn. 8:46).

[15] John Henry Newman, "The Dream of Gerontius," in *The Dream of Gerontius and Other Poems* (London: Oxford University Press, 1914), 6.

[16] Saint Cyprian of Carthage, *On the Unity of the Church*, no. 6, as quoted at http://www.ccel.org/fathers2/ANF-05/anf05-111.htm.

longs to wed this world to God's own Word, the sheer self-utterance of Trinitarian love. "By communicating His Spirit," declares *Lumen Gentium*, "Christ made His brothers, called together from all nations, mystically the components of His own Body."[17]

So, by all means, take up the text of the Church's dogmatic constitution *Lumen Gentium*. Read the inspired language of the Bride in conversation with her Spouse. Then, see if the spiritual juices do not at once start to flow. Look to the Bride whom Christ has filled with the riches of His glory; look to her who is the very prolongation of His presence in history, her to whom we owe every good thing in heaven and on earth.

---

[17] Second Vatican Council, *Lumen Gentium*, no. 7.

CHAPTER VI

A FINGERNAIL'S OPENING TO FAITH

There is a wonderful moment in a little-known novel by Henry James called *Roderick Hudson*, in which a young man from New England, bent on escaping his Puritan past, wanders into the baroque stillness of Santa Cecilia, one of Rome's most beguiling and luminous churches. There he meets the maddeningly beautiful Christina Light, whose charms have enraptured all of Rome. Neither, of course, has come to pray. Determined dilettante that he is, Rowland Mallet has come merely to muse, filling the emptiness of an afternoon with the usual woolgathering of the idle aesthete. It was said of John Ruskin that he knew the use of everything in a church except the altar. It could be said of young Mallet that concerning churches he saw the paintings, but missed their purpose. "Rowland walked to the altar, and paid, in a momentary glance at the clever statue of the saint in death, in the niche beneath it, the usual tribute to the charm of polished ingenuity."[1]

And Miss Light? Lapsed Catholic that she is, poor Christina has quite forgotten how to pray. And so they fall into desultory conversation, which James, the master storyteller, renders as follows:

> "I am afraid I am sadly prosaic," he said, "for in these many months now that I have been in Rome, I have

---

[1] Henry James, *Roderick Hudson*, in *Henry James: Novels 1871-1880* (New York: The Library of America, 1983), 345.

never ceased for a moment to look at Catholicism simply from the outside. I don't see an opening as big as your finger-nail where I could creep into it!"

So what does this young man believe, she asks?

"Please tell me about your religion."

"Tell you about it? I can't!" said Rowland, with a good deal of emphasis.

She flushed a little. "Is it such a mighty mystery it cannot be put into words, nor communicated to my base ears?"

"It is simply a sentiment that makes part of my life, and I can't detach myself from it sufficiently to talk about it."

"Religion, it seems to me, should be eloquent and aggressive. It should wish to make converts, to persuade and illumine, to sway all hearts!"[2]

She's dead right, of course. Faith seen simply from the outside, lacking even a fingernail's opening to its mysteries, is no good to anyone. If to give the thing expression, you have got first to unearth it from the bottom of your trunk, of what use is that? Even Miss Light, for all that she's managed to squander of her own faith, even she knows what it's for: to be communicated. When handed a lighted lamp, one does not put it under a bushel basket.

Ah, but there is irony here of which neither the two characters, nor, for that matter, the author himself, Henry James, who imagined the scene, insinuating all the vaunted subtlety of his intelligence into it, seem the least bit aware. And that is the startling and vivid presence of the young

---

[2] James, *Roderick Hudson*, 347-48.

martyr, Cecilia, whose finely sculpted figure beneath the high altar forms the backdrop to this scene of highly stylized chatter. Features which, on closer inspection, will reveal the deep wound from the Roman sword which repeatedly fell across her neck.

Is it not odd that in the bright shadow of this sainted woman's tomb, so expressively adorned by the marble figure above the vault containing her incorrupt remains, the action of the other two should unfold? Or should one say inaction? For like the frivolous women in T. S. Eliot, who "come and go / Talking of Michelangelo,"[3] they betray not the slightest curiosity concerning the quality of *her* faith, which so moved her to suffer and die in its behalf. If we must make a defense to those who call us to account for the hope that is in us (cf. 1 Pet. 3:15), we could do far worse than to draw upon the life and example of this young woman, whose extraordinary serenity of soul the artist Maderno sought four centuries ago, when her tomb was reopened and the beauty of her incorrupt body inspired a memorable poem in stone. Here, to be sure, was someone who saw things unfailingly from the inside, who would never have stood stammering about, wondering just where at the bottom of her trunk lay the mystery of the universe. Indeed, the Mystery itself having laid hold of her, Cecilia's story becomes one of consummate sanctity, and unending bliss and joy.

"There is only one unhappiness," cries Leon Bloy, "and that is—not to be one of the saints."[4] There can be no object more lovely, nor perfection more pure, than that of sanctity, hitting the bull's-eye of beatitude. "Of all great

---

[3] T. S. Eliot, "The Love Song of J. Alfred Prufrock," in *The Complete Poems and Plays: 1909-1950* (New York: Harcourt, Brace & World, 1971), 4.
[4] Leon Bloy, *The Woman Who Was Poor* (New York: Sheed & Ward, 1939), 356.

hearts," writes Henri Gheon in *The Secret of the Cure d'Ars*, "the greatest is still the heart of a saint. For it wants to contain not only its neighbor, strangers, all suffering, sinful, warring humanity—but God Himself."[5] So how many Catholics these days are aspiring to become saints? Are you, dear reader? Am I? Is anyone interested in cornering that particular market? Where is the motive force for martyrdom most in evidence these days? In parishes?

"Men's curiosity searches past and future," writes Eliot in the *Four Quartets*:

> And clings to that dimension. But to apprehend
> The point of intersection of the timeless
> With time, is an occupation for the saint—
> No occupation either, but something given
> And taken, in a lifetime's death in love,
> Ardour and selflessness and self-surrender.
> For most of us, there is only the unattended
> Moment, the moment in and out of time,
> The distraction fit. . .[6]

To be fair, I suppose, to those of us caught in the web of so many unattended moments, there is the question, well, How the deuce does one witness to Christ in a Church where so few appear even to believe in Christ? If current surveys are to be trusted, more than half the number of Catholics polled do not accept Church teaching on the Holy Eucharist. They do not, in a word, believe in the Real Presence of our blessed Lord hidden beneath the outward show of bread and wine.

---

[5] Henri Ghéon, *The Secret of the Curé D'Ars* (New York: Longmans, Green and Co., 1929), 7.
[6] Eliot, *Four Quartets*, in *The Complete Poems and Plays*, 136.

Is this, I wonder, an acceptable level of apostasy? Are our spiritual lords prepared to countenance so fundamental a departure from the rule of faith? Surely denial, or even diminished ardor, concerning so central an axiom of Catholic belief amounts to the profoundest unsettling of the deposit of faith itself. What else does it mean when confusion about the Eucharist becomes endemic, if not the unraveling of Christianity itself?

The crisis is precisely and most deeply ecclesiological, since the Eucharist is at the very core of who the Church is and what she is for. "Christ warns us that we must answer for what we have received," writes François Mauriac. "When it is Himself we have received, what shall we not have to answer for?"[7]

"What is lacking [in the Church today]," laments Luigi Giussani, founder of Communion and Liberation, "is not so much the literal repetition [of the Christian message] as the experience of an encounter."[8] Unless the encounter with grace takes place, the graced encounter with Christ, no amount of institutional change or adaptation will make the slightest difference in people's lives. In the presence of Christ, in Whom "all the fulness of God was pleased to dwell" (Col. 1:19), anything and everything may become an evocation of Him. Nothing need escape this all-encompassing horizon of His life, the lines from which literally intersect at every turn. Not even our sins can avert His gaze. "Man," declares Angelo Scola (now patriarch of Venice) in a wonderful metaphor, "the image of God, is a

---

[7] François Mauriac, *The Eucharist: The Mystery of Holy Thursday*, trans. Marie-Louise Dufrenoy (New York: Longmans, Green and Co., 1944), 56-57.
[8] Rev. Msgr. Luigi Giussani, VII Ordinary General Assembly of the Synod of Bishops, in "Thirteenth General Congregation," *L'Osservatore Romano*, 26 October 1987, p. 3.

simple silhouette which finds its luminous figure only in Christ";[9] we are the shadow of which He is the substance.

Jesus Christ is the effulgence of the Father. God's own appearance among men, His "monstration" before the world, His possession of me, His laying hold of my life, becomes nothing less than a springboard into God's life, a miracle of divinization. "Who could ever speak of love to the man possessed by Christ, overflowing with peace?"[10] to quote Dionysius the Areopagite. A man literally does not know even his own longing, the seething *eros* of his own soul, until he meets Christ, in that sudden awakening of grace and glory encountered in the smile of Another. This truth of Christ bears transcendent witness, it carries conviction in every line. Indeed, says Giussanni, "Christ's message is so much in keeping with what man longs for that the individual who hears it cannot help being struck by it."[11] A man could no longer live, were he never again to hear His voice, never again to see His face.

But really, who nowadays is actually struck by it? Where is this acute longing being felt to see God's face? If the Christian religion is nothing less than an entirely new, totally unsurpassed event in human history, ought not every effort to be made to acquaint Christians with that event, with the One Who comes to meet us in this graced encounter? Christ brought all things new by bringing

---

[9] Patriarch Angelo Scola, *Hans Urs von Balthasar: A Theological Style* (Grand Rapids: Wm. B. Eerdmans, 1995), 49.

[10] Dionysius, quoted in "Notes from a Talk by Msgr. Luigi Giussani at the International Meeting of Communion and Liberation Leaders in August 1989," in *Communion and Liberation: A Movement in the Church*, ed. Davide Rondoni (Montreal: McGill-Queen's University Press, 2000), 122.

[11] Rev. Msgr. Luigi Giussani, *L'avvenimento cristiano* (Milan: BUR, 1993), 29-50, as quoted at http://www.comunione-liberazione.org/UK/txtuk/00/testo1bis.html.

Himself,[12] Saint Irenaeus reminds us. In the circumstance, is it too much to ask that, at the very least, Christians themselves show some lively curiosity concerning the character of this blessed event?

And where else but in the context of every local Church does one actually encounter the event of Christ, or even knowledge of His Word? How is it possible, I am saying, for people to countenance Christ while at the same time dismissing the only surviving profile we possess of Him, namely His Church? In the final analysis is it not the Church we must thank for the gift of God made man? Years ago in a wonderful passage by de Lubac I came across, but which, alas, continues to elude me, this great man of the Church framed the question in exactly that way: "For us Jesus is living. But under which sandhill would, perhaps not His name or memory, but His living influence, the effect of the Gospel and of faith in His divine Person, lie buried, were it not for the continuity of His Church? Without the Church, Christ would be bound to evaporate, crumble, become extinguished. And what then would mankind be, were Christ to have been taken from them?"[13]

---

[12] "What then did the Lord bring us by His advent?—Know ye that He brought all [possible] novelty by bringing Himself." Saint Irenaeus, *Against Heresies*, bk. IV, chap. XXXIV, no. 1, as quoted at http://www.ccel.org/fathers/ANF-01/iren/iren4.#html section 34.

[13] Indeed, the terms of the proposition being interchangable, what would the Church be without Christ? In a stunning passage from *The Splendor of the Church*, in my judgment the most luminous treatment of the Church ever written, de Lubac does not hesitate to confess the fact that were she not what she claims to be, that if the faith proclaimed by Peter on the road to Caesarea were not her faith, "I should not wait for her to deceive me at the human level before I separated from her. For in that case not all her benefits on the human level, nor all her splendor, nor all the riches of her history, nor all her promise for the future, would be able to make up for the dreadful void at the heart of her." In short, if Christ be not the source of her splendor, there can then be no alternative but to condemn the squalor. See Henri Cardinal de Lubac, S.J., *The Splendor of the Church* (San Francisco: Ignatius Press, 1986), 219.

Divest Christ of His Body, that Body which is the Church, I am saying, and all at once He floats haplessly away into realms of pure ozone, leaving the world untouched by grace, unmoved by the wonder of salvation wrought by the flesh that Christ took on. "The flesh is the hinge of salvation,"[14] exclaimed the fiery north African, Tertullian. It is, therefore, the purpose of the Church to anchor Christianity to this most solid earth, the world's body, thus preventing faith from flying off into vaporous abstractions that can do us no good whatsoever. Instead, they leave us prey to a species of Platonism that cannot finally satisfy, because in bypassing the world's body, it fails to redeem one's own.

It is this elementary fact which we find right at the beginning of our reflection on the Church: namely that she alone is Christ's Body, through whom salvation is to be mediated to the world. She is thus the means chosen by God for the world's salvation. By her relationship with Christ, says *Lumen Gentium*, the Church "is in Christ like a sacrament or as a sign and instrument both of a very closely knit union with God and the unity of the whole human race. . ."[15]

This must be the fundamental datum for which the Church is prepared fearlessly to go to the wall, to defend in every age, but especially in the present situation of arrant disbelief. With so much ersatz spirituality in the air, so many rarefied souls bent on finding bliss beyond the basic structures ordained by Christ, the Church more than ever is needed to rivet man's attention to the real. There can be no

---

[14] Tertullian, *De resurrectione*, 8, 2, in Catechism, no. 1015.
[15] Second Vatican Council, Dogmatic Constitution on the Church *Lumen Gentium* (November 21, 1964), no. 1.

ultimate opposition between Christ and His Church, if only because the Church exists to convey the entirety of God's Word and Sacrament across the span of the centuries. "Established by Christ as a communion of life, charity and truth, [the Church] is also used by Him as an instrument for the redemption of all, and is sent forth into the whole world as the light of the world and the salt of the earth."[16]

More to the point, Christ's Church holds the key to that necessary unity of office, which legitimizes Word and Sacrament. In other words, that chord of Catholicity in which the strands of office, Word, and Sacrament all intersect, is precisely what ties the Church to Christ. Lacking that essential unity of office, that divinely instituted structure of authority on which both Word and Sacrament depend, what claim has the Church to commend her message to the world? Unless Peter speaks with the accent of Christ (When the Pope speaks it is Jesus Himself whom we hear,[17] says Saint Catherine of Siena), what is left to validate the exercise of authority? The Church can neither proclaim Christ in Word, nor celebrate Him in Sacrament, if she does not already possess Him in the very unity of office.

She is, accordingly, the keeper of the tablets, and they all are inscribed with His name. Like a good wife wedded to her husband, she speaks only of Him, Who is Christ. What else finally matters? Thanks to the Church, writes Mauriac, "a certain Word has come down to us, not as a memory, not as something that can be called to mind, but as something

---

[16] *Lumen Gentium*, no. 9.

[17] Cf. *Catherine of Siena: The Dialogues*, trans. Suzanne Noffke, O.P. (New York: Paulist Press, 1980), 214-15. Here she repeatedly refers to the pope as "Christ of earth," a designation of which she is especially enamored.

active and living: 'Your sins are forgiven you.' 'This is my body given for you.'"[18]

Isn't this, finally, the point? Isn't this the issue on which everything else turns, the fact of a divinely constituted Church whose power to confect the Eucharist for the world's salvation, is nothing other than a share in God's own holiness? "I am no longer troubled by any of the criticism leveled at the human organization of the Church," says Mauriac. "The worst of what I discover there in the past or of what I observe today still leaves me indifferent because the Church constitutes for me the entirety of the human means used by grace to fecundate each of the souls who have recourse to that source of living water impounded at Rome."[19]

I mean, isn't this the heart of the matter? Suppose one were someday to stumble upon an organization so structured as to be able to impart real life to its members, eternal, unending life to anyone who cared to sign on, with so many crooked lines suddenly made straight. Would not one's first impulse be that of gratitude, thanksgiving? A sense of continual, stunned gratitude would surely overwhelm the beneficiary of such a gift. Who, after all, can forgive himself? Or vouchsafe communion, or everlasting life? One might as well expect the Baron von Munchausen to pull himself up out of the bog by his own beard!

"Many Christians today give the impression that they do not feel at ease in the Church," wrote Jean Cardinal Daniélou a quarter century ago in *Why the Church?*

---

[18] François Mauriac, *What I Believe*, trans. Wallace Fowlie (New York: Farrar, Straus and Company, 1963), 5.
[19] *What I Believe*, 6.

and that they only remain faithful to her with difficulty. I must say that my experience is contrary to theirs. The Church has never disappointed me. It is rather I who would be inclined to accuse myself of not having drawn profit enough from all that she had to offer me.[20]

How utterly ungenerous, it seems to me, for people who stand to gain so much from the gift of the Church, to choose instead to ridicule and revile the giver. Few things are more abject or unchivalrous. Is it not tantamount to an attack upon one's own Mother? How can God overlook so depraved a disregard for not just our own Mother Church, whom He gave us to honor and love, but His Mother Mary as well? Let us then turn with gratitude and love to the Church from whom we received so much, including the promised salvation she mediates, and endeavor to return something of our own as well.

---

[20] Jean Cardinal Daniélou, S.J., *Why the Church?* (Chicago: Franciscan Herald Press, 1975), 141.

CHAPTER VII

THE PEARL IS NOT THE OYSTER'S MISTAKE

I once heard a great story about a group of tourists wandering through Saint Peter's Basilica, their attention fixed on the expert guide ushering them from one immensity to another. Finally, following an exhaustive demonstration of so much grandeur and magnificence, the learned fellow turns to the group to ask if there are any questions. Only one: How much does it weigh?

What a priceless moment that must have been! How completely it reveals the prevailing mindset, the rampant reductionism of which would have us measure the total worth of a building solely in terms of the accumulated weight of wood and mortar and marble poured into it. So vulgar a preoccupation would doubtless have parlayed all the oceans white with foam into so much commercial salt, or the beauty of Niagara Falls into a hydroelectric plant, or the marvels of the Grand Canyon into a mining operation intent on extracting all the ore. And what, pray, might we have made of the pearl in the oyster? A mistake? I rather suspect, by the way, that the one who asked the question was probably the same chap who, surveying the ruin of Rome's Colosseum, dismissed it in the end on the ground that, lacking a roof, it was obviously unfinished.

So what is Saint Peter's for? Has it any use apart from the income that accrues to it as a tourist attraction? For that matter, what is any church for? Forget the sumptuous baroque pile across the Tiber, its vast interior echoing with the tramp of tourists—what about the banal clapboard structure across the street, its boring interior stripped of statuary and, not infrequently these days, its Eucharistic Presence confined to a broom closet? Indeed, what is the point of Christianity that we should require churches in which to confect its mysteries?

"The work of art has no purpose," pronounces Guardini in a wonderful essay called *The Playfulness of the Liturgy*. No, but it does possess a meaning, namely that it should be, and that in its being, its existence, "it should clothe in clear and genuine form the essence of things."[1] Its existence, there-fore, is entirely subordinate to the splendor, the glory and the radiance of the truth—the *splendor veritatis*—of which it happens to be the enfleshment.

Granted, then, that is what churches are for. And when liturgy, the supreme work of art, is rightly understood, it escapes the necessity of having to justify itself in relation to anything other than itself. Certainly, argues Guardini, "it does not exist for the sake of humanity, but for the sake of God. In the liturgy man is no longer concerned with him-self; his gaze is directed towards God. In it man is not so much intended to edify himself as to contemplate God's majesty"[2]—again, the triumph of being over doing, logos over ethos, and yes, prayer over politics (even if, as Cardinal Daniélou put it in one of the most provocative books I ever read, a book which literally worked a sea change in my own mind, we need to think of prayer as a political problem[3]).

---

[1] Rev. Romano Guardini, *The Playfulness of the Liturgy*, in *The Church and the Catholic & The Spirit of the Liturgy* (New York: Sheed & Ward, 1953), 175.

[2] *The Playfulness of the Liturgy*, 177-78.

[3] Jean Cardinal Daniélou, S.J., *Prayer as a Political Problem* (New York: Sheed and Ward, 1967).

But who really cares nowadays? In lines of disturbing resonance from a poem called "Church Going," the English writer Philip Larkin explores that very question. Of course, given Larkin's lethal pessimism about most everything, the answer he comes up with does not inspire much confidence about why anyone should bother going to Church at all. Still, he often does go and is much vexed and puzzled as to why:

> Wondering what to look for; wondering, too,
> When churches fall completely out of use
> What we shall turn them into, if we shall keep
> A few cathedrals chronically on show,
> Their parchment, plate and pyx in locked cases,
> And let the rest rent-free to rain and sheep.
> Shall we avoid them as unlucky places?
>
> Or, after dark, will dubious women come
> To make their children touch a particular stone;
> Pick simples for a cancer; or on some
> Advised night see walking a dead one?
> Power of some sort or other will go on
> In games, in riddles, seemingly at random;
> But superstition, like belief, must die,
> And what remains when disbelief has gone?
> Grass, weedy pavement, brambles, buttress, sky . . . [4]

Alas, Larkin's answer leaves very little in the way of hope for human beings bent on finding belief. With cheerless certitude, he predicts "[a] shape less recognizable each week, / A purpose more obscure,"[5] causing him at last to wonder

---

[4] Philip Larkin, "Church Going," in *Collected Poems* (London: Marvell Press, 1988), 97-98.
[5] "Church Going," 98.

who might finally be the last, the very last, to seek out such places for what they once were.

But, again, what is that shape or purpose? What is the point of the thing? I remember how greatly struck I was on first coming across Chesterton's observation about Saint Francis, that it was never Christianity that he loved, but only Christ.[6] And where else but in Christianity, in the faith and the churches adorning the hills and valleys of his beloved Umbria, would he have found Him? Where, indeed, but amid the picturesque ruin of San Damiano, a shrine in Assisi to which Francis would often go to pray before the crucifix, would Christ find him? There and in many other churches that mark the landscape of the Church's institutional life, Francis and Christ would find each other. Isn't that the motive force behind the love he exhorted others to offer to priests everywhere—that here is the interface between earth and heaven on which, finally, everything in the universe depends?

Summoned once to a village by a group of irate church-goers, their priest having repeatedly given them scandal, Francis flat out refused to join in condemning the fallen cleric. Instead, he walked over to him and, kneeling to kiss his hands, declared: "I do not wish to consider sin in them [priests] because I discern the Son of God in them and they are my masters. And I act in this way since I see nothing corporally of the Most High Son of God in this world except His Most holy Body and Blood which they receive and which they alone administer to others."[7]

---

[6] G. K. Chesterton, *St. Francis of Assisi* (London: Hodder and Stoughton, 1923), 17.

[7] Saint Francis of Assisi, *The Testament*, nn. 9-10, in *Francis and Clare: The Complete Works*, trans. Regis J. Armstrong, O.F.M. Cap., and Ignatius C. Brady, O.F.M. (New York: Paulist Press, 1982), 154.

Isn't that a stirring testimonial to the office of priest instituted by Jesus Christ? Apart from that which exists to make Christ present, that is, the Church and the holy priesthood He instituted, none of us would ever find his way safely home to Christ. Certainly, Francis himself could not possibly, but for the fact of the Church herself, have found his own sublime vocation, given him through her, to rebuild the Church Christ suffered to redeem. "He will do these things when he is in love,"[8] comments Chesterton, fingering the pulse of an extravagant outpouring of sanctity, which has come to define the charism of *il poverello* (little poor man). It is the key to everything, and only in the Church does one find it to unlock the heart of the Beloved.

"Even the saints are tainted by daily sins," Augustine tells us. "The whole Church cries: 'Forgive us our sins!' She is, therefore, blemished and wrinkled (Eph. 5:27). But through contrition these blemishes are removed, these wrinkles smoothed away. The Church's unceasing prayer is one of contrition that she may be made pure. And so it will remain until the end of time."[9]

It is the central paradox of her life, that she who dispenses the medicine of divine mercy is herself sorely in need of the same. Here I often think of a letter from Flannery O'Connor, written with the most wonderful trenchancy and wit to an agnostic friend then struggling mightily with the question of the Church (the only "The Church," the comedian Lenny Bruce used to say, only he wasn't being funny). She wrote, "I think that the Church is the only thing that is going to make the terrible world we are coming to

[8] Chesterton, *St. Francis of Assisi*, 16.
[9] Cf. Saint Augustine, *The Correction of the Donatists*, in *Nicene and Post Nicene Fathers*, 1st ser., vol. 4, ed. Philip Schaff (Peabody, Mass.: Hendrickson Publishers, 1994), 647.

endurable; the only thing that makes the Church endurable is that it is somehow the body of Christ and that on this we are fed."[10]

Isn't that stunning? She has nailed the point precisely: Only Christ can save, only He can deliver us from a world determined on doing us in. And the Church? She is worth saving, worth belonging to (that is, endurable) only to the degree that, in some finally mysterious way, the whole blessed Body of Christ becomes identifiable with her, because, O'Connor says, "on this we are fed." In other words, if Christ be the fulcrum lifting the world onto the plane of grace and glory, the purpose of His Church is to prolong that elevation in every age and place until the final trumpets summon us all home. She is the keeper of the tablets, and each bears His name, and more: She is custodian of the Eucharist, which bears His being.

Here, to be sure, is the real stone of stumbling, the stiletto point of scandal, which, nevertheless, and quite impossibly it seems, Christ asks us to impart to the world. It is on this point that both the meaning of the basilica in Rome, and every church building in communion with Rome, is meant to converge. For in the end, everything is reducible to what Balthasar, in as noble and forthright an effort as I know to return to the source, the point of origin, has called "the ineffable poverty of the divine, incarnate, crucified love."[11] At the heart of the Church it is not *what* we find that matters, but *Whom*, namely Christ, the Second

---

[10] Flannery O'Connor, *The Habit of Being* (New York: Farrar, Straus and Giroux, 1979), 90.

[11] "Today we must investigate in what way the Christian wealth, without losses— such as a vanquished army leaves behind on the battlefield—relates to its origin: to the ineffable poverty of the divine, incarnate, crucified love." Rev. Hans Urs von Balthasar, *Convergences: To the Source of Christian Mystery*, trans. E. A. Nelson (San Francisco: Ignatius Press, 1983), 12.

Person of the Trinity, Who longs for an encounter with us in the sacrament which is His Church.

Like the Beloved Disciple who saw the risen Christ on Easter morning, and thus believed, we, too, must see in order to believe. Unless we see evidence of the Son of God in the radiant smile of the mother (His and ours), who will believe that the Father sent Him to be our Savior? That He *is* present there for us to see is precisely the catechesis our time needs if it is to overcome the facile reductions so beloved by ideologues, that is, those who would strip the Body of Christ of its supernatural life, pursuant to this or that secular, bourgeois model of management and manipulation. What could be worse than to divest Christ's Bride of all possible connection with her Spouse, refusing even to honor that transcendence towards God which is the distinctive mark of her hope? To pretend somehow that her nature and work exclude the business of mystery, that we may bypass the plane of bedrock altogether, is to do a terrible violence to her very soul, her finality before God. Such depredations deny the Church her primary focus, which, if it is anything, is Trinitarian and christological— or it is nothing at all.

Isn't this what really happened in the aftermath of the council, in the bitterness of debate between the partisans of Chapter II of *Lumen Gentium*, with their fashionable image of "the People of God," which can at once arouse and legitimize dreams of empowerment (as seen for example, in misinterpretations of the phrase, "We are the Church!"), and the partisans of Chapter III, who, alas, given their widely caricatured status as doddering old clerics, would certainly be expected to resist, in a spirit of sullen reaction, the triumphant march of time, with its promised dawn of a new age blessedly free of antique episcopal fixations on power and privilege—not to mention, of course, the myriad leveling effects of all this vaunted democratization, most particularly in the area of catechetics, which has so poisoned the air of religious education for a generation or more?

And yet, curiously enough, had not both sides quite forgotten, in their unseemly obsession with the machinery of the Church (Who gets power to do what to whom?), to fasten both chapters, that is, the Church as People of God and the Church as hierarchy, to the real meaning of the text found in Chapter I of *Lumen Gentium?* There the architects of genuine renewal were to lay out in the most luminously precise way an understanding of the Church as mystery, as that mystery of communion with the Triune God mediated in and through the Person of Christ, and only then diffused out into the world He suffered to deliver from the scourge of sin.

It would seem thus a matter of supreme importance that the Church rediscover herself as mystery in her transparency before the Lord. Questions of power in the Church are simply a vast and boring exercise in futility, utterly distracting to men and women intent on a life of holiness. "Be worthy of the flame consuming you,"[12] urges the poet Paul Claudel, who certainly meant by that something less managerial than Marian. Who more than she stood in silent, adoring receptivity before the Word, the Incarnate Word Whose unfolding she patiently awaited at the center of a pure and virginal heart?

So here we are some forty years after the Second Vatican Council, and the silly season seems to go on and on forever.

---

[12] Paul Claudel, prologue to *The Tidings Brought to Mary* (Chicago: Henry Regnery Company, 1960), 19.

Really, there is no apparent abatement in sight. The landscape remains fairly strewn with the wreckage of entire communities of priests and religious, of demoralized laity wandering about in still-pained bewilderment at the dismemberment of their faith. What went wrong?

Could it be that the crisis has come about because all the main questions, the truly compelling questions, got shoved aside in the mad rush to welcome the world into the sanctuary of holy Church? Questions of Trinitarian and christological moment, for example, whose answers could then give rise both to an ecclesiology faithful to Christ, and to a set of pastoral initiatives faithful to the Church, never really entered the post-conciliar consciousness. And yet, we all know, if only as an intuition reaching right down to the bottom of our Catholic being, that in matters of faith no river can ever be divided from its source, nor presume to rise above its source; that no moral precept can derive from something other than dogmatic principle; that being is prior to doing; and that the very Logos of God possesses a primacy over every expression of human ethos. (Remember the warning issued by Cardinal Journet that "Jesus saved us by being what he was before saving us by doing what he did"?)[13]

Surely this is why, in becoming forgetful of that Source, we inevitably lose our way, diverted into some quite meaningless backwater that goes exactly nowhere. Examples, unfortunately, abound—from the endless, sterile agitation

---

[13] Charles Cardinal Journet also notes here: "The action of Christ flows from the being of Christ. The being of Christ exists for the sake of his action, not like a means for an end, but like a spring with respect to its overflowing." *The Primacy of Peter: From the Protestant and from the Catholic Point of View*, trans. John Chapin (Westminster, Md.: The Newman Press, 1954), 34.

over the ordination of women, on over to the current state of liturgical experimentation, which seems almost laughably to beg the question of what the Mass is for. Chesterton's quip concerning the predicament of modern man leaps to mind here. Having invented the loudspeaker, he suddenly realized he had nothing to say.

Have we anything to say? If so, it is only because we heard it first from Him, through her, in the place where the Bride eternally speaks His name.

CHAPTER VIII

DRY STONES, STONY HEARTS

Midway through the final episode of Francis Ford Coppola's epic screen masterpiece, *The Godfather*, an aging and ravaged Michael Corleone surveys the moral wreckage of his world. The surviving head of an utterly corrupt family crime syndicate, he suddenly awakens to the need to confess his sins.

But it has been thirty years or more since his last Confession; and in light of the usual Mafia depredations along the way, he believes himself to be quite beyond the pale. "What is the point of Confession," he tells the old archbishop, "when you've no desire to repent?" Still, he remains acutely haunted by his many sins, particularly the treacherous killing of a once beloved brother. "I hear you are a practical man," the wise archbishop reminds him. "What have you got to lose?"

Indeed, what *has* he got to lose? Are mass murderers less in need of God's mercy? What, for that matter, has any of us to lose in exchange for the momentary wrenching of the sacrament—our sins? But of course! And in the moment or two it might take to divest our souls of them, a sentence of death has been lifted. What sort of price is that? Who in his right mind would not at once forego an eternity of loss, including the unspeakable loss of the very One for Whom we were made, in return for his miserable sins? To escape the deadly snare of the Devil—to quote the old *Penny*

Catechism, on which so many cradle Catholics of my generation first cut their teeth—whose whispered pleasures
turn to dust and ashes the moment we give into them, I
should think one would do almost anything. Faced with an
outbreak of plague, one does not disdain the doctor whose
syringe brings relief. Confession for the Catholic is medicine for the soul; it is the necessary serum without which
recovery is not possible. And where else but holy Church
does one go to receive this gift, this incomparable medicine
of mercy?

So where have all the Confession lines gone? Why are so
few disposed to tell their sins, and thus to encounter the
shattering event of Christ's mercy and forgiveness? "Blessed
be sin," writes Bernanos in his classic *The Diary of a Country
Priest*, "if it teaches shame."[1] Nowadays, it would seem, we
sin without shame.

And if it is really God Himself Who comes to meet us in
this sacrament of the Church, this sacredly terrifying mystery in which, alone with the Alone, we feel the action of
His mercy, why are we not falling all over one another to get
into the box? How far we have come from the case of the
paralytic described in the Gospel of Saint Mark (cf. Mk. 2:4-
12)! So eager is this man to experience the healing touch of
God that he enlists four men to help lower him through the
roof of the home where Jesus is staying. And what does Jesus
do? On seeing such faith, the Son of Man not only remits his
sin but restores him to health as well. All were astounded,
reports Mark, and they go away giving glory to God. "We
never saw anything like this!" they all exclaim (Mk. 2:12).

---

[1] George Bernanos, trans. Pamela Morris, *The Diary of a Country Priest* (New
York: Macmillan Company, 1937), 124.

Are we nearly as hungry to be made whole as the paralytic was? And to think, moreover, that besides forgiving the sins we commit, He quite forgets them as well. "I will not remember your sins," He tells us in Isaiah 43:25. Flabbergasting. Here God's memory appears to be rather poorer than our own; we tend not to forget sins, especially those committed by others. It reminds me of the story of the fellow who claimed to have seen God face to face. Informing his pastor of the fact, the latter instructed him to ask God to reveal the secret sins of his heart (evidently the pastor had several) and to let him know, the next time they met, what they were. So the fellow duly asks God, Who at once tells him, "I cannot remember."

In every event of Confession in which we tell the priest our sins, it is God Himself Whom we encounter. It is the time and place where, in the unsurpassed language of Eliot's *Four Quartets*:

> The wounded surgeon plies the steel
> That questions the distempered part;
> Beneath the bleeding hands we feel
> The sharp compassion of the healer's art
> Resolving the enigma of the fever chart.[2]

So, once again, why are all the lines outside the confessional empty? Why the seeming abandonment of the practice of auricular confession in so many parishes in this country? I say "seeming" because while most parishes will not actually forbid penitents from going to Confession, they not infrequently schedule them at a time when the

---

[2] T. S. Eliot, *Four Quartets*, in *The Complete Poems and Plays: 1909-1950* (New York: Harcourt, Brace & World, 1971), 127.

window, as it were, of opportunity is pretty nearly shut: twenty minutes, say, before the Saturday evening Mass. The great mystic and doctor of the Church, Saint John of the Cross, describes the soul as "undergoing a cure, in order that it may regain its health—its health being God Himself."[3] Yet, judging from the habits of most modern Catholics, there are no illnesses of the soul, no enigmas to be resolved; the only maladies are material, for which the prescribed solution is pharmacological.

Who knows, perhaps we are in the midst of an outbreak of virtue of such cosmic proportions that the scourge of personal sin may be said to have been wiped clean away—that despite every appearance of living in an age twisted all out of joint, replete with grotesqueries of every sort, a veritable blizzard of blessedness has swept over us, leaving a sort of sinful remnant, I suppose, a handful or so of neurotically scrupulous souls, in need, not of Confession, but of therapy. Spare me the penance, Father; just send me a pill. Is that, I wonder, the sign of the times we've been waiting for?

Meanwhile, on a less sentimental showing, one could read the situation very differently. For instance, it could certainly be argued that the incidence of sin remains pretty much equally horrific in every age, but with this striking difference: Our own age has grown more or less accustomed to the fact. We've happily come to terms with sin and iniquity. When temptation strikes, we're rather like Oscar Wilde: We get over it by simply giving in to it. Peering deep into the same abyss our ancestors (who rightly recoiled before its hellishness) faced, we, in our facile

---

[3] Saint John of the Cross, *The Dark Night of the Soul*, trans. E. Allison Peers (New York: Image Books, 1959), bk. 11, chap. XVI, no. 10.

sophistication, have turned it all into a theme park. Call it nihilism without the abyss. In short, we've learned to domesticate our despairs.

And isn't this, as Kierkegaard reminds us in *The Sickness unto Death*, the hidden face of every expression of despair, that it is precisely unaware of being in despair?[4] The man in its grip remains so sunk in everydayness that the demon needn't announce himself as having already taken up residence in his heart. And if sin persists, what then? Well, it certainly needn't be remedied by so patently medieval an exercise as regular Confession—or, indeed, through any sort of priestly mediation with all the clanking machinery of a suspect Church getting in the way. In the way of what? Why the endless odyssey of the self-centered self, whose solitary quest for ultimate meaning and salvation loftily refuses the least institutional intrusion. Christ's Body, the Church, which we know in faith He fashioned in order to carry us all to Heaven, is nowadays quite widely perceived as the principal barrier to grace, this agent of tyranny intent on destroying the soul of the spiritual man.

The problem, of course, is that salvation is not a self-help enterprise; still less is it based on entitlement. As for the charge that the machinery of priestcraft keeps getting in the way of individual men and women bound for glory, it does not follow that once the mediation is dismantled true reform will automatically happen, since one has only substituted one's own sinful self for so-called institutional sinners. "Search for the perfect Church if you will," warns Father

---

[4] Cf. Søren Kierkegaard, *The Sickness unto Death* (Princeton, N.J.: Princeton University Press, 1980), 45.

Andrew Greeley, "when you find it, join it, and realize that on that day it becomes something less than perfect."[5]

No, the mystique of the totally privatized religion intent on reaching God in ways wholly devoid of material mediation, intolerant therefore of any and all institutional interference, leads not to life, but lunacy. ("Shall I tell you where the men are who believe most in themselves?" asked Chesterton of the smug publisher who fatuously believed otherwise. ". . . [I]n lunatic asylums.")[6] As Flannery O'Connor once noted in an essay from her book, *Mystery and Manners*: "When Emerson decided, in 1832, that he could no longer celebrate the Lord's Supper unless the bread and wine were removed, an important step in the vaporization of religion in America was taken, and the spirit of that step has continued apace. When the physical fact is separated from the spiritual reality, the dissolution of belief is eventually inevitable."[7]

What other way had God in mind to reach us if not through the body of this world? We're certainly not saved by angels. Why, He even prepared a womb for His Word, the womb of one younger than sin, Bernanos tells us, through whom salvation has come to the world.[8] As Eliot writes in *Ash Wednesday*:

> And the light shone in the darkness and
> Against the Word the unstilled world still whirled
> About the centre of the silent Word.[9]

---

[5] Rev. Andrew Greeley, "Why I Remain a Catholic," in *Why Catholic?*, ed. John J. Delaney (Garden City, N.Y.: Image Books, 1980), 63.

[6] G. K. Chesterton, *Orthodoxy* (New York: Dodd, Mead and Company, 1946), 22.

[7] Flannery O'Connor, *Mystery and Manners* (New York: Farrar, Straus & Giroux, 1969), 161-62.

[8] Bernarnos, *The Diary of a Country Priest*, 212.

[9] Eliot, "Ash Wednesday," in *The Complete Poems and Plays*, 65.

We have become lost, anorexic souls, untethered to the body of this world—like the ancient philosopher Plotinus, who would not give out his own address, so ashamed was he to be in the body. The sad fact is, we Catholics have more and more lost the sense of sacrament, the intuition that the world is a wedding, joined to God in Christ, Whose Bride is the Church made lovely by His Blood. Perhaps this is why, to quote Cardinal Ratzinger, "The sense of the scandal through which a man can say to another man, 'I absolve you from your sins,' must be rediscovered."[10]

Still, if the Church wishes to survive, to recover even something of that original intensive energy with which she subdued an entire pagan world, then the abuse must once more give way to the use. To this end she must recognize that it is only because of the absolute "I" of Jesus Christ, pronouncing in authoritative accent *His* Word of forgiveness, and not the personality of the priest (the latter having most wonderfully withdrawn into the objective impersonality of Christ), that the very possibility of the remission of sin exists at all. For this reason, as *Lumen Gentium* reminds us in its robust restatement of the traditional teaching of the Church, every priest acts in the very person of Christ, Who remains *the* High Priest of the New Covenant. In putting on Christ in this most intimate and efficacious way, priests assume the very ontology by which He exercised His ministry on behalf of sinners. "By the power of the sacrament of Orders, in the image of Christ the eternal high Priest, they are consecrated to preach the Gospel and shepherd the faithful and to cel-

---

[10] Joseph Cardinal Ratzinger with Vittorio Messori, *The Ratzinger Report* (San Francisco: Ignatius Press, 1985), 57.

ebrate divine worship, so that they are true priests of the New Testament."[11]

As a very holy priest once put it, sounding the depths of the mystery of divine mercy, "When our Lord looks on a sinner, he isn't a sinner; he used to be." Who in his right mind could ever imagine confessing his darkest and most humiliating secrets—withheld even from his spouse!—to anyone other than Christ? "After such knowledge," asks Eliot, "what forgiveness?"[12]

How painfully clear it has now become, following history's most bloody-minded century, that until a lively sense of sin is restored—*and* that supernatural representation of Christ upon which the Catholic priesthood finally depends—no recovery of spiritual health, to say nothing of heroic sanctity, will be possible. Despite resolute and repeated calls to universal holiness, to sound the tocsin of the conciliar event issued a generation ago, unless we Catholics return in great numbers to the practice of penance, the Church in this country will slip unnoticed into a state of complete inanition, and where then will the Christian be who needs her in order to find Him?

Like everything else bearing on Catholic belief and practice, the problem is finally christological. It isn't confession we're losing an awareness of, it is Christ. In the Roman courtyard where Michael Corleone and the saintly old archbishop meet, the latter removes a stone from the fountain and, looking at it closely, explains how for centuries it has been lying there inert in the water. "But the water has not penetrated it. Look," he says, "it is perfectly dry. The

---

[11] Second Vatican Council, Dogmatic Constitution on the Church *Lumen Gentium* (November 21, 1964), no. 28.

[12] Eliot, "Gerontion," in *The Complete Poems and Plays*, 22.

same thing has happened to men in Europe. For centuries they have been surrounded by Christ. But Christ has not penetrated, Christ doesn't live within them."

And does He live any more convincingly within us? Are our hearts less stony than theirs? We have, it seems, all grown more or less impenetrable to Christ, who has loved us (says Pascal) even more ardently than we have loved our sins; and whose courtship of us has been so madly insistent that those same sins are now nailed to His Cross.[13] Small wonder, then, that we should likewise prove so impenetrable to His Bride, the Church, who speaks His Word, wishing only to prolong His merciful presence into the heart and soul of our humanity.

---

[13] Blaise Pascal, "The Mystery of Jesus," in *Pensées*, trans. A. J. Krailsheimer (New York: Penguin Books, 1966), 315.

CHAPTER IX

TO HELL WITH
THE SYMBOL

It was only later, at the party thrown in my son's honor, that I tried telling him how the experience he'd gone through was, to put it mildly, the most sublime moment of his life. Even were he to cross Pikes Peak on a pogo stick, go over Niagara Falls in a barrel, or land on Uranus under an umbrella, nothing could ever equal the importance of the event of that morning.

He grinned sheepishly, reacting altogether as I expected any normal nine-year old would, the transistor wires trailing from one ear (firstfruits of a proud father's largess), the other meanwhile cocked against the current of whatever piety he figured was coming. Instead, taking his hand, the one the priest had placed Holy Communion in for the first time not one hour before, I returned to my place, acutely mindful of my own inadequacy.

Well, what do we say, anyway, to the very young who come innocent and wide eyed to the sacrament, this central ritual of our Catholic-Christian faith? I know well enough what we *do*: We give them things—transistor radios, for instance. We give holy things, too: books and rosaries and holy cards which, after a decent interval, are seldom seen again.

But what actually do we tell them about this mystery of the Body and Blood, Soul and Divinity of Jesus Christ? What do we say about *this* gift, which more than any other, forms the whole basis of Catholic identity, igniting the spark of that divine conflagration Christ came into this world to set? Here, after all, is the irreducibly unique symbol of our faith, deeply rooted in God's own Word, the supreme drama of Whose death on the Cross brings life to the world.

Do we ever attempt an inventory of the cost borne by the Son of God to enable us to receive Him in Holy Communion? Never mind the inestimable good it does us— what was the price exacted of Him, the endless and terrible scandal of a God who freely dies to feed us, breaking Himself for bread? "Many people think that it is simply up to them to reconcile themselves with God," declares Balthasar, "and that many do not need such reconciliation at all. . . . They have no conception of the flames necessary to burn up all the refuse that is within man; they have no idea that these flames burn white hot in the Cross of Jesus. There is a cry that penetrates all the cool pharisaism of our alleged religiosity: 'My God, my God, why have You forsaken Me?' In the darkest night of the soul, while every fiber of His body is in pain, and He experiences extreme thirst for God, for lost love, He atones for our comfortable indifference."[1]

Let's face it, here is the most fearful and holy of all the mysteries in which our lives as baptized children of God are centered. It is the only mystery, moreover, in which the unseen Lord of the universe—the ineffably transcendent Other—freely consents to become wholly present in an act of perfect, unsurpassed self-donation. Who among us is equal to an event as august as this?

> Down in adoration falling,
>   This great Sacrament we hail;

---

[1] Rev. Hans Urs von Balthasar, *"You Crown the Year with Your Goodness": Radio Sermons*, trans. Graham Harrison (San Francisco: Ignatius Press, 1989), 79.

Over ancient forms of worship
   Newer rites of grace prevail;
Faith will tell us Christ is present,
   When our human senses fail.[2]

All that we believe and understand of the faith handed
on to us from the apostles—they in turn having received it
from the hands of Christ—is to be found in the Church
herself, sacramentally inscribed in the rituals of her
everyday life. This means, most especially, in the liturgy,
where, for the generality of believing Catholics, the
encounter with Christ most frequently takes place. Here
we celebrate the whole rhythmic ebb and flow of Christ's
own life, the yearly cycle of Annunciation, Nativity,
Baptism, Transfiguration, Passion, Death, Descent,
Resurrection, Ascension, Pentecost, not to mention the
promised Parousia to come when, on the other side of
history, Christ will return in glory.

These are real historical events we remember; it is not an
idea or abstraction whose commemoration we are charged
with observing. But what happens when we gather together
to celebrate these mysteries of the life and death and
Resurrection of Christ? What is the extraordinary discovery
that we make? It is nothing short of miraculous. In our very
remembrance of these events, we rejoice to find that, far
from merely reminding ourselves of yet another anniversary,
it is in the very nature of the events themselves to re-present
once more, in the present moment, all that they are, that
once again, and in the most vivid and vibrant way, they are
made real and efficacious for God's People. Here is a com-

---

[2] Saint Thomas Aquinas, Hymn for the Solemnity of the Most Holy Body and
Blood of Christ *Pange lingua gloriosi*.

pletely fresh and contemporaneous retelling, reshowing, of an ancient and saving event. "Do this in remembrance of me" (Lk. 22:19), insists Jesus. "Do this for an anamnesis of Me," and—bingo!—the bread and the wine mixed with water become God's very Body.

The words of Christ graven upon the formula of institution are so utterly unequivocal as not to permit any escape whatsoever. How can this be? Only because it is God Himself instituting it, indeed, with such scandalous intent that the sign and the thing signified by it have become one and the same. The bread is not some vague representation of Christ; it is, rather, the purest re-presentation of Him. Bread becomes God's very Body, offered up to the Father for the world's salvation. Never mind that the whole paschal event occurred a long time ago in a faraway place: it is now contemporaneous with all time and every place, because in the sudden wake of Christ's Resurrection, His smashing through the grave and the gate of death, all time has been overcome. The finite structures of temporality, in short, have been reconfigured in an altogether new and radical way. Time itself, as the Pope reminds us in *Tertio Millennio Adveniente*, has become a dimension of eternity.[3]

The Mass, therefore, is a memorial of a very special and singular kind. Man may do the remembering, but the reality he remembers is no longer in the past but here, now, always. The Church's memory thus begets a Presence which, dissolving at one stroke that distant historical landscape in Palestine, places us in direct sacramental proximity with the mystery itself. It is not like a trip down memory lane where imaginatively one tries to enter into the music of long

---

[3] Pope John Paul II, Apostolic Letter on Preparation for the Jubilee of the Year 2000 *Tertio Millennio Adveniente* (November 10, 1994), no. 10.

ago, nor is it like the family of a deceased relative, when its members long to see their dear departed once again and by a sheer act of will summon the shade from the netherworld. The dead do not return; but Christ did and continues to do so at every Mass. Otherwise, of course, the blessed apostles who knew Jesus intimately would, by virtue of the immediate physical proximity to Him, put the rest of us at an infinite and fatal disadvantage. Yet we have it on faith, and as a result of the Mass, that we may enter into a living communion with Christ equal to that of God's own Mother and His closest disciples. As the Catechism puts it, "Christ enables us *to live in him* all that he himself lived, and *he lives it in us*. 'By his Incarnation, he, the Son of God, has in a certain way united himself with each man'" (no. 521, citation omitted, emphasis in original).

Nevertheless, how dismayingly silent we are on the subject! We speak hardly a word in praise—to say nothing of defense—of the Eucharist, by which we are defined and made one. If being a Catholic means anything, it surely means eating God's Body and drinking His Blood. It all begins with God's total gift of self unto death, which beckons us to what we call the life of grace and charity.

But if the figures are to be believed, more than 70 percent of all Catholics either cannot identify or do not agree with the Church's teaching on Christ in the Eucharist.[4] Meanwhile, how many of us feel any urgency to set them straight? And is our reluctance to do so tantamount to admitting the absurdity of the teaching?

So what becomes of a Church whose heart is adjudged empty by so many? When the one thing that alone makes

---

[4] Gallup Poll, 1992, cited at http://catholicapologetics.com/ba3.htm.

everything else in Catholic Christianity worth preserving is no longer perceived to be there, or believed in, what are we left with—an empty cistern? "And upside down in air were towers," writes Eliot in *The Waste Land*, "Tolling reminiscent bells, that kept the hours / And voices singing out of empty cisterns and exhausted wells."[5]

We are witnessing the drying up of faith and the worship of false gods, sheer idols of usury and lust and power. "[F]or my people have committed two evils," says the Lord God to the prophet Jeremiah; "they have forsaken me, the fountain of living waters, and hewed out cisterns for themselves, broken cisterns, that can hold no water" (Jer. 2:13).

Certainly, no one's coming to Mass to hear the homily. We are not saved by a preacher; only God can save us. And when we disdain the gift of His Body vouchsafed in the Holy Eucharist, what hope have we of salvation?

The poet Hopkins, it seems to me, has caught the necessary distinction here, namely that there are those for whom the Eucharist is only an "interesting uncertainty," and those for whom it must always remain a complete if "incomprehensible certainty."[6] On which side of the divide do we find ourselves? And then there is my absolute favorite: Flannery O'Connor's wonderfully fierce reply to Mary McCarthy, the famous novelist and lapsed Catholic, whose eccentricities on the subject of the Eucharist had quite succeeded in reducing the Incarnate Word to the status of mere symbol, "Well, if it's a symbol," young Flannery thundered, "to hell with it."[7]

---

[5] T. S. Eliot, *The Waste Land*, in *The Complete Poems and Plays: 1909-1950* (New York: Harcourt, Brace & World, 1971), 48.

[6] Rev. Gerard Manley Hopkins, S.J., *The Letters of Gerard Manley Hopkins to Robert Bridges*, ed. Claude Collier Abbott (London: Oxford University Press, 1935; revised 1955), 187-88.

[7] Flannery O'Connor, *The Habit of Being* (New York: Farrar, Straus and Giroux, 1979), 125.

The fact that Protestants would shrink in honest horror from a reality concerning which most Roman Catholics today remain fearfully indifferent surely reveals the distance we've come. This is the great difference that separates us from the sensibilities of first century Catholics, who evinced so lively an awareness of the reality of Christ's presence in the Eucharist. "I have no delight in corruptible food," wrote the impassioned Ignatius, bishop and martyr of Antioch, to the Church at Rome, where he would shortly be thrown to the beasts. "I desire the bread of God, the heavenly bread, the bread of life, which is the flesh of Jesus Christ, the Son of God, who became afterwards of the seed of David and Abraham; and I desire the drink of God, namely His blood, which is incorruptible love and eternal life."[8] Is this the stuff of sanctity, or what?

"The Church in early days," writes Louis Bouyer, "had an awareness which we have lost (but which we can regain) of the unity which unites all the sacraments in one single reality, the heart of which is the Eucharist."[9]

Is it possible that today's legion of lapsed Catholics now constitutes one of the largest single denominations in this country? The Church must clearly be disintegrating in our midst if the defining feature of membership is increasingly a loss of faith in its core belief. After all, the nexus struck by Christ between His Eucharistic and ecclesial Body is central to the faith we profess. Everything points to a study of the relation between the two, as Henri de Lubac reminds us: "Each has been entrusted to the other, so to speak, by

---

[8] Saint Ignatius of Antioch, *The Epistle of Ignatius to the Romans*, chap. VII, as quoted at http://www.newadvent.org/fathers/0107.htm.

[9] Rev. Louis Bouyer, C.O., "Que Signifie la Confirmation?" in *Paroisse et Liturgie* (n.p., 1951), 6, quoted in Henri Cardinal de Lubac, S.J., *The Splendor of the Church* (San Francisco: Ignatius Press, 1986), 148.

Christ; the Church produces the Eucharist, but the Eucharist produces the Church."[10]

I wonder if most of us do not sometimes feel embarrassment in the presence of this loftiest of the sacraments, which literally consummates all the others and to which they are all ordered. The Eucharist, says Vatican II, is that which is both source and summit of the entire Christian life.[11] Again, do we not often act as if silence regarding this most foundational reality of the Roman Catholic Church were, in fact, the preferred way? I mean, of course, among the 30 percent who actually claim to believe? And yet such silence can never be permissible for the Christian.

For myself, in thinking of this deep, most necessary mystery of faith—the one mystery Christ assured us would always remain the hardest saying of all—three things seem especially evident. First, we can never say enough about the Eucharist. Like any great love, we shall never come to an end of, never fully account for, nor exhaust, the ground of our devotion. Second, we hardly ever say anything at all about this truth on which, manifestly, so much lasting happiness depends. "When we get down to bedrock," de Lubac tells us, citing Saint Thomas, "*there* is contained the whole mystery of our salvation."[12] And, third, it is all simply too important to be left to the nuns and priests to say everything about it (or to the theologians, for that matter, who in their learned and clever way will not infrequently etherealize the reality of Christ's Eucharistic presence altogether). Are we not all called to be saints? And how does sanctity happen, apart from this Body on which we are fed?

---

[10] De Lubac, *The Splendor of the Church*, 134.
[11] Cf. Second Vatican Council, Dogmatic Constitution on the Church *Lumen Gentium* (November 21, 1964), no. 11, in Catechism, no. 1324.
[12] De Lubac, *The Splendor of the Church*, 148, emphasis added.

I like to think that this is rather what the poet Charles Péguy had in mind when, at the turn of the last century, he declared that the real revolutionaries of the coming age would be the parents of Christian children. Indeed, Péguy further noted that there were only two sorts of people at the heart of Christendom, the saint and the sinner, and that the transition from one to the other was a work of grace, of which the Eucharist remained *the* supremely efficacious example.[13]

Heaven knows, we've certainly had quite enough ersatz revolutionaries produced by that bloodiest of centuries. Isn't it about time we Christians took up the challenge posed by Christ, the perfect Revolutionary, to eat His Body and drink His Blood, the platform, as it were, from which we are all to be launched into that deep space which is Heaven?

---

[13] "I am a sinner," he would unfailingly confess. "I am not a saint. The saints are immediately recognizable. I am a good sinner. A witness. A sinner who attends Sunday Mass in the parish, a sinner with the treasures of divine grace." Indeed, having thus described himself, he would then add: "No one is as competent as the sinner in the matter of Christianity. No one except the saint . . . they are generally one and the same person. The sinner and the saint are two integrating elements, so to speak, or two integrating parts of the mechanism of Christianity. Together, each vital to the other." Gianni Valente, "Péguy on the Threshold," in *What Counts Is the Wonder* (Rome: 30 Days Books, 2002), 31.

CHAPTER X

NIGHT HAS FALLEN, NOBODY NOTICED

Not long ago, my wife and son arrived at a doctor's office for a routine appointment, only to be driven out into the hall to escape the onslaught of daytime TV. Great, steamy discussions of sex had evidently supplanted the usual reruns of *Romper Room* and *I Love Lucy*—not marital sex, mind you, in which the fruits of lovemaking include life, but sordid, unwholesome sex, wholly deranged from either life or love. It was an interview show, featuring a couple of call girls exclaiming delightedly about the commercial advantages of selling themselves, especially to clients of considerable discretion and cash. Flesh being just another commodity, they reasoned, why not market it like any other upscale consumer item?

What was most instructive about the episode, it turns out, was not the ardor of the ladies. After all, sex being their business, one might expect a certain Rotarian pride in performing it well. No, the really striking thing about the entire discussion was the complete absence of any objection from the studio audience, not to mention the poor souls in the doctor's office who, by turns, found themselves assaulted and seduced by it. Not a whisper of horror or disapproval from either group concerning a way of life which, let's face it, has been fairly widely adjudged to be squalid and degrading. Curious.

Do you see the problem we're up against here? It is not that sin doesn't in fact exist, or that people who traffic in it cannot become shameless, but that no one seems to mind. How many churchgoing Catholics do you suppose were in that audience? Why weren't *they* mobilized to act? Does it matter?

Well, as a matter of fact, it does. It matters a lot. The Church, you see, is very clear about our need—that is, the laity's need—to give witness in the world to all that transcends the world: the value of purity, for example, or chaste love. These are among the things of God that even daytime TV ought not to trash. "[T]he Lord wishes to spread His kingdom also by means of the laity,"[1] says *Lumen Gentium* in the chapter dedicated to the importance of the role and mission of the lay state. "The faithful, therefore, must learn the deepest meaning and the value of all creation, as well as its role in the harmonious praise of God. They must assist each other to live holier lives even in their daily occupations. In this way the world may be permeated by the spirit of Christ and it may more effectively fulfill its purpose in justice, charity and peace."[2]

In this way, the council reminds us, the world will be filled with the spirit of Christ, and in those annealed (as it were) to Him "will Christ progressively illumine the whole of human society with His saving light."[3]

In other words, we Catholics are obliged, precisely as Catholics, to protest, even in the secular order, such abuses as routinely assault our sensibilities. "[E]ven in secular business there is no human activity which can be withdrawn

---

[1] Second Vatican Council, Dogmatic Constitution on the Church *Lumen Gentium* (November 21, 1964), no. 36.
[2] *Lumen Gentium*, no. 36.
[3] *Lumen Gentium*, no. 36.

from God's dominion."[4] And a line or two later, parsing the crucial distinction, the council fathers declare: "For it must be admitted that the temporal sphere is governed by its own principles, since it is rightly concerned with the interests of this world. But that ominous doctrine which attempts to build a society with no regard whatever for religion, and which attacks and destroys the religious liberty of its citizens, is rightly to be rejected."[5]

A public life, the Church is saying, in which there is no reference to God, no cathedral spire to elevate the souls of men, is an inhuman place to be. Faith is not anchored solely to the future; it is a defining feature of this life as well. Nor is it merely an exercise of the interior life, as though the realm of culture had nothing to do with giving shape to the soul. Indeed, were the sacred and secular to move in altogether separate spheres, their orbits never to converge along the axis of the human, man would be reduced to a dualism so complete as to sunder his very self. "If we accept a complete dissociation of the sacred and profane worlds," warns Jean Cardinal Daniélou in his moving little book, *Prayer as a Political Problem*, "we shall make access to prayer absolutely impossible to the mass of mankind. Only a few would be able to find God in a world organized without reference to Him."[6]

Could it be, however, that Christianity and the Church simply don't matter very much anymore, that the supernatural no longer exists as an order of reality commanding social significance—like the scene from the famous Federico Fellini film, *La Dolce Vita*, featuring an enormous statue of

---

[4] *Lumen Gentium*, no. 36.
[5] *Lumen Gentium*, no. 36.
[6] Jean Cardinal Daniélou, S.J., *Prayer as a Political Problem*, trans. J. R. Kirwan (New York: Sheed and Ward, 1967), 35.

San Salvador fastened by ropes to a helicopter moving across the skyline of a modern Italian city, and nobody noticing the hovering symbol of their salvation? Is that it, I wonder? On the other hand, what does the world really know of the faith which it finds so little reason not to abhor, particularly if the only available evidence around is other Christians, the example of whose lives may not be enough to convict them of being Christians? It is not that the ideals of Christ have been tried and found wanting, to recall a line from Chesterton, but that having been found difficult, they were simply never tried.[7]

Is that why we have grown so callous to the corrupting effects of sin, so demoralized by the disorder around us, that none of it matters anymore, that not even the trumpet blast from the council itself, summoning us toward "the sanctification of the world from within as a leaven,"[8] can arouse us from our bourgeois slumbers?

I write "bourgeois," not out of contempt for middle-class values, but because that is what becomes of faith when it ceases to exact demands from those who practice it, and when it does not offer anything distinctive to the world it is expected to try to convert. More and more, it now seems, we live amid the fleshpots of Egypt, that lotus land of postmodern suburban cheer, heedless of the abyss into which we are about to fall. Some years ago, for instance, a jury in Pittsburgh finally reached its verdict concerning a group of young women (several of them ex-students from the university where I teach) brutalized by local police in an

---

[7] G. K. Chesterton, *What's Wrong With the World* (New York: Dodd, Mead and Company, 1910), 48.
[8] Second Vatican Council, *Lumen Gentium*, no. 31.

Operation Rescue attempt some years before. Their judgment: None of the brutality mattered in the least. The jury, in the words of the plaintiff's attorney, "believed everything the women said, but they didn't find that it shocked their conscience." And why is that? Because, she concluded, "What can shock your conscience if you watch TV?"

Of the twelve who voted to acquit, in effect declaring storm-trooper tactics permissible since we have grown so used to them on TV, how many do you suppose would call themselves Catholic, subject, therefore, to higher standards than those shown on network television?

Meanwhile, rock star Marilyn Manson, *the* quintessential symbol of popular culture's slide into a cesspool of depravity, continues to be the rage among the under fourteen set. Deliberately affronting the sensibilities of mainstream parents—many of whose children may be seen flocking to his concerts wearing T-shirts festooned with Satanist slogans ("American by Birth, Antichrist by Choice," is a particular favorite)—a recent album, "Antichrist Superstar," has lately become something of an anthem of teenage angst.

So where, in the name of God, are the parents of these children? Are any of them Catholic? And if so, what has become of the hope that is in them (cf. 1 Pet. 3:15)? Or have they converted it into the cheap coin of the secular realm, whose false gods leave them empty in the end, like the fabled figure who traded his gold for a horse, a cow, a goose and, finally, a whetstone, which he soon threw into the water thinking at last he'd secured the precious gift of freedom, only to discover, of course, once the false euphoria left him, the emptiness of exchange.

Is that what we have come to, I wonder: so much gold given away for one miserable whetstone that is then given away as well? The council fathers warn, "Let them not, then, hide this hope in the depths of their hearts, but even in the program of their secular life let them express it by a continual conversion and by wrestling 'against the world-rulers of this darkness, against the spiritual forces of wickedness.'"[10]

Without this hope, are we not similarly sunk in the same quagmire of corruption as the purveyors of a culture bent on suicide, destruction, and disease? How often one is haunted by the question once put by Albert Jay Nock: How, he asked, can a civilization know whether or not it has fallen into a Dark Age?[11] The answer: When the lights have all gone out, no one notices the darkness. Have they gone out? Has anyone noticed?

More and more, we have got to face the fact that we cannot save this civilization, cannot arrest its accelerating descent into barbarism. Only God can. A people besotted for a generation or more on images of deviance, violence, and depravity cannot even be trusted to keep the machinery going, much less the meaning of a civilized order. Yet it is not our job to shore up human civilization. Ours is to try and sanctify our souls, and those of our children, pursuant to which civilization may or may not be saved. A people bent on saving the world without first looking inward to try to save its soul will certainly fail to save either. Our first task, then, is to renew the interior life, permitting a shaft or two of God's light to penetrate our own darkness. Then, and only then, will the encircling gloom and dark outside perhaps begin to fall away.

---

[10] Second Vatican Council, *Lumen Gentium*, no. 35.

[11] "I once thought it would be amusing," he wrote, "to attempt an essay on how to go about discovering that one is living in a dark age." Albert Jay Nock, quoted in William F. Buckley, Jr., *The Unmaking of a Mayor* (New York: Viking Press, 1966), 168. Nock died in 1945, so perhaps his assessment of the intervening half-century would deepen even his strain of congenital pessimism.

"Lead, Kindly Light," wrote Newman in 1833. "[A]mid the encircling gloom, / Lead Thou me on!"

> The night is dark, and I am far from home—
>   Lead Thou me on!
> Keep Thou my feet; I do not ask to see
> The distant scene—one step enough for me.[12]

Without question, this has been the message of Vatican II. There in the document on the Church, the lay members of Christ's Mystical Body are enjoined "by their very vocation, [to] seek the kingdom of God by engaging in temporal affairs and by ordering them according to the plan of God. They live in the world, that is, in each and in all of the secular professions and occupations. They live in the ordinary circumstances of family and social life, from which the very web of their existence is woven."[13]

In short, the building up of the world, its growing conformity to Christ, is a task which necessarily includes the layman and his family, through which, as Pope John Paul II has often reminded us, the future of man and his world pass.[14]

It is also and finally the lesson of the saints, of holy men like Benedict of Subiaco, whose flight from the corruptions of the world into the mountain fastness outside Rome, there

---

[12] John Henry Newman, "The Pillar of the Cloud," in *The Dream of Gerontius and Other Poems* (London: Oxford University Press, 1914), 141.

[13] Second Vatican Council, *Lumen Gentium*, no. 31.

[14] Indeed, this very theme, that man, in the relations that shape the fabric of his life, is the way chosen by Christ for the Church to follow in its path toward the Kingdom, was first struck by Pope John Paul II in his Encyclical Letter at the Beginning of his Papal Ministry, *Redemptoris Hominis* (March 4, 1979), no. 14. "Man," he wrote, particularly in that primal community in which the whole network of relationality is grounded (i.e., the family), "is the primary and fundamental way for the Church."

to commune with God, attracted such attention to his fierce, single-minded joy that it soon drew others to a common life of faith. Thus began a great movement whose lasting fruit would be the Christianization of the West. It is certainly the lesson of Vatican II, where the marching orders for an empowered laity are set out: "Each individual layman must stand before the world as a witness to the resurrection and life of the Lord Jesus and a symbol of the living God."[15]

There is no reason why a Christian civilization, a Catholic Christendom, cannot be fashioned anew, but not without saints determined to blaze the trail that others will follow. It is the great paradox of history, notes Chesterton, "that each generation is converted by the saint who contradicts it most."[16] His job is to restore the world to sanity, to what the statesman Edmund Burke called "the decent drapery of life,"[17] highlighting by the heroism of his example the virtues the world will no longer esteem. There can be no substitute for the witness of holy men and women. The rebuilding of a ruined world will begin when enough people fall to their knees, their minds undistracted by the fate of the world, their hearts set on the love of God, the life of His Church.

---

[15] Second Vatican Council, *Lumen Gentium*, no. 38.
[16] G. K. Chesterton, *St. Thomas Aquinas* (New York: Sheed & Ward, 1933), 8.
[17] Edmund Burke, *Reflections on the Revolution in France* (Garden City, N.Y.: Doubleday & Company, 1961), 90.

CHAPTER XI

WHY NO RELISH FOR RAPTURE?

It has not often been noted—the news for the most part having been conveniently suppressed by his liberal hagiographers—but Angelo Roncalli, throughout his brief five-year stint as John XXIII, remained a fairly traditional pope. Indeed, by today's politically correct standards, we should probably have to dismiss his entire pontificate as dangerously reactionary. (I can see them now, splashed across the pages of the *National Catholic Reporter*: lurid references to a "deeply suspect" pontiff.)

Besides issuing a spate of pious encyclicals on such shopworn topics as the Rosary, penance, and priestly perfection, Blessed John XXIII intervened at the council on behalf of his beloved Saint Joseph, ordering that his name be inserted into the canon of holy Mass—hardly the stuff of liberal legend, I'd imagine.

And such was the ardor of his longing for the Church's final consummation, her glorious and triumphant deliverance on the far side of history, that he personally insisted on including chapter seven of the conciliar text on the Church, which contains some of the most profound and rich scriptural meditations on "The Eschatological Nature of the Pilgrim Church and Its Union with the Church in Heaven." The chapter title nicely suggests the sort of otherworldly tone of the thing, don't you think? Here is how it begins: "The Church, to which we are all called in Christ Jesus, and in which we acquire sanctity through the grace of God, will attain its full perfection only in the glory of heaven, when there will come the time of the restoration of all things. At that time the human race as well as the entire world, which is intimately related to man and attains to its end through him, will be perfectly reestablished in Christ."[1]

How exactly do we know this? Because Christ, lifted high above the earth, to recall the famous Johannine text, will draw all men to Himself (cf. Jn. 12:32), and because the Body He fashioned for this work, the efficacious extension of His own Person in the world, Mother Church, has told us it is so. She who is the realization in this world of God's final irrevocable covenant with man, she who is founded on the grace of One Who loves and accepts her unconditionally— her testimony must be holy and true. She is not bound, as was Israel, by the limitations of a Law she cannot keep; her status as Bride, as most favored daughter of God, does not depend on the maintenance of an ethos borne by fallen men, but on the absolute love of the divine Logos Himself. It is the sheer stubborn persistence of that grace, the free bestowal of that irrevocable love, that alone sustains her. Thus the Church, God's very Bride wrapped in deepest mystery, exists precisely in order to raise the world to the dignity of a Christian sacrament. In point of fact, "as the universal sacrament of salvation,"[2] to quote *Lumen Gentium*, she has no other task in time to perform.

When the pope speaks, declared Saint Catherine of Siena, it is Jesus Himself Whom we hear.[3] Here the theo-

---

[1] Second Vatican Council, Dogmatic Constitution on the Church *Lumen Gentium* (November 21, 1964), no. 48.
[2] *Lumen Gentium*, no. 48.
[3] Cf. *Catherine of Siena: The Dialogues*, trans. Suzanne Noffke, O.P. (New York: Paulist Press, 1980), 214-15.

logical tradition of the great saints speaks with one voice. It does not murder to dissect. The martyred Joan of Arc, for example, patroness of France, would not countenance any confusion on that score. When truculent and deceiving judges sought at her trial to force the issue, she would not bend to their wishes, insisting instead that she loved both Christ and the Church. Her wily enemies then redoubled their efforts to trip her up. "You constantly contradict yourself!" they exclaimed. "Is it Jesus you believe and love above all? Or is it the Church you believe and love above all?" All this only exasperated her. "It seems to me that it is all one, Christ and the Church, and that we ought not to make any difficulty of it."[4]

Does it surprise anyone that the company of those holding to this position includes among its ranks some of the greatest names in modern Catholic theology? Karl Rahner, for instance, in the last years of his life, confessed that,

> for me all the anger is in the end secondary. When I affirm that, in what in the strict sense is called "Church," I hear in a believable way the absolute promise of God in which he says to me in Jesus Christ, crucified and risen, "In the absolute power of my love I communicate myself to you and that for all eternity," then measured by that everything else is secondary. Then I experience my life as a waiting for the fulfillment of this absolute promise in which God guarantees not this or that but Himself, the absolute God, the incomprehensible one, and forever. Given this is it difficult to understand that for me everything of a negative nature that I experience and suffer in the Church is of secondary concern? . . . In the face of negative experiences the

---

[4] Saint Joan of Arc, quoted in Henri Cardinal de Lubac, S.J., *The Splendor of the Church* (San Francisco: Ignatius Press, 1986), 212.

question is very quickly asked: Shall I still remain in the Church? The question drives me "crazy." For me as a believer it is in the last analysis meaningless. What can the word "still" mean here? It is like asking whether I will "still" be a human being, or whether I will "still" live in this pitiable twentieth century.[5]

It is fortifying, I find, to read such words. Written by one whom liberal Catholicism would seek to co-opt as necessary to its own dissent, the passage puts completely to flight the conceits of those who imagine the faithful as having invariably to choose, say, between private conscience and Catholic creed, when, in actual fact, the terms of the dialectic simply will not fit. The Church is not a debating society, whose members attempt, in the spirit of John Stuart Mill, to mediate the inevitable clash of opinion, splitting the difference, as it were, between this or that disputed doctrine of the faith. A membership organized along those lines could doubtless draw upon many different kinds of recruits, but none of them would be the least bit interested in finding salvation through forensics. No, the Church as a window looking on the face of God, or a highway leading to Him, is not in the business of debate but deliverance. As the place in time where Heaven and history intersect, where we locate the final and unsurpassed eruption of grace in nature, salvation in space, the Church necessarily precludes there being any other place or time outside of or beyond herself. To bear witness to God, to His Word made flesh—one can only do this in the Church He built upon the grace of the rock called Peter.

---

[5] Rev. Karl Rahner, S.J., *Faith in a Wintry Season: Conversations and Interviews with Karl Rahner in the Last Years of His Life*, ed. Paul Imhof and Hubert Biallowons, trans. ed. Harvey D. Egan (New York: Crossroad, 1991), 142-43.

"[T]he promised restoration which we are awaiting," to take up the theme once more from *Lumen Gentium*, "has already begun in Christ, is carried forward in the mission of the Holy Spirit and through Him continues in the Church. . ."[6] The eschatological age, I am saying, has already dawned, thrust into time by the event of Christ, carried now mysteriously along by His Church. The world's future having been placed in redeemed relation to God the instant Christ burst the bonds of sin and death, we are thus trained to see, amid even the finitude of this world, the beginning of "a new heaven and a new earth" (Rev. 21:1).

"Already the final age of the world has come upon us," the council fathers remind us, "and the renovation of the world is irrevocably decreed and is already anticipated in some kind of a real way,"[7] even as the Church, languishing in this vale of tears, outwardly indistinguishable from a world destined to pass away, takes her pilgrim place among men who must travail in exile and pain before the promised revelation of the sons of God (cf. Rom. 8:19-22).

But who any longer believes this, or is equal in hope to the vision of faith it holds out? "[W]e seek the city which is to come" (Heb. 13:14), declares the author of the Letter to the Hebrews. "I am the resurrection and the life," says Jesus, "he who believes in me, though he die, yet shall he live" (Jn. 11:25). Yes, but it is all too often only the earthly city, the place where the fleshpots beckon, that holds in thrall the heart of man, which is why, to recall C. S. Lewis's magnificent sermon preached amid the darkest days of World War II, "[Y]ou and I have need of the

---

[6] Second Vatican Council, *Lumen Gentium*, no. 48.
[7] *Lumen Gentium*, no. 48.

strongest spell that can be found to wake us from the evil enchantment of worldliness which has been laid upon us for nearly a hundred years."[8]

What a strangely perverse silence fills the air the moment the subject of Heaven comes up! Is it not strange that while all the ancient peoples incessantly reflected on the nature of the next world, having shrewdly intuited the impermanence of this one, scarcely any self-respecting modern appears the least bit interested in the "hereafter"? How seldom, for example, we think of death, an event that, after all, represents the real point of entry into eternity. *Respice finem*, which means "look to the end," is an ancient pagan motto whose message the Church early on embraced. Christ Himself enjoined His disciples to watch and wait, mindful of the end: "Therefore you also must be ready; for the Son of man is coming at an hour you do not expect" (Mt. 24:44).

Holy Church continues to repeat the stern reminder: "Since however we know not the day nor the hour, on Our Lord's advice we must be constantly vigilant so that, having finished the course of our earthly life, we may merit to enter into the marriage feast with Him and to be numbered among the blessed. . . ."[9]

And yet, again, it would appear that for most self-styled enlightened folk, death and the world to come are hardly the things at which they care to look right now. The irony of course is that by the time they finally do turn their minds to the end, it may very likely be the end. "Human kind cannot bear very much reality,"[10] says T. S. Eliot.

---

[8] C. S. Lewis, *The Weight of Glory* (Grand Rapids: Macmillan Company, 1949), 5.
[9] Second Vatican Council, *Lumen Gentium*, no. 48.
[10] T. S. Eliot, *Four Quartets*, in *The Complete Poems and Plays: 1909-1950* (New York: Harcourt, Brace & World, 1971), 118.

Given the extent of modern man's flight from death, from the "hereafter," one has got to ask whether the human hunger for Heaven, for that blessed state which even now directs the Church's trajectory in time, across the sea of history, hasn't become some sort of vestigial organ. Is it possible, I am asking, for the wings of the human spirit to atrophy for want of use? Nowadays, to speak of man's pilgrim status, of his promised homeland in Heaven, of the travail of the world and hope for life beyond the grave, is to invite a blank stare of stupefaction among the many for whom eternity has lost all attraction.

And not only self-confessed moderns suffer from this loss of attraction for Heaven. In Dom Hubert van Zeller's delightful memoir, *One Foot in the Cradle*, he describes a conversation with Monsignor Ronald Knox, his great friend, who despite the clearest possible evidence of impending death, continued to hold out against the end. "In the train he told me he had no wish to die. 'One clings,' he said, 'and I can't think why. You would have thought anyone would prefer heaven to fruit juice.'"[11]

Heaven's a nice place, no doubt, but nobody seems in a great hurry to get there. This quite astonishing fact is the result, it seems to me, of a couple of influences, which together have conspired to undermine genuine hope in and longing for the afterlife. First, there are the seductions of secularity, which undeniably weigh upon the world. Such delectations induce a certain amnesia concerning the last things, most especially that eschatological horizon about which the Dogmatic Constitution on the Church speaks so eloquently. What is under attack here is the purpose of life

---

[11] Rev. Hubert van Zeller, O.S.B., *One Foot in the Cradle* (New York: Holt, Rinehart and Winston, 1966), 242.

understood and lived out against a backdrop ultimately beyond life.

Second, there is the frequent and astounding insipidity of so much that passes for the joys and delights of Heaven. Call it the sentimentalization of paradise. That, too, works against an interest, both abiding and real, in anyone wanting to go there.

"If I had to sum up the crowds I have talked to on street corners in the last forty years," Frank Sheed reminisced near the end of a life marked by an amazing amount of evangelism, "I would say that practically nobody wants to go to Heaven. I don't mean that I myself am at this moment anxious to leave this world and be on my way to the next. But all the same I do see Heaven as a place of great joys. Most people apparently don't."[12]

For too many of us, I'm afraid, the only idea we have of Heaven is the everlastingly boring one of people seated forever on a cloud playing harps and shouting hosannas. Imagine, if you can bear it, the prospect of an eternal guitar Mass, accompanied by the St. Louis Jesuits singing, "Yahweh, I Know You Are Near." Such visions reduce eternal life to what Sheed calls a "supertechnicolor church service"[13]—let's face it, a pretty miserable compensation for all the sins we fear we shall have to give up in order to get there.

How bracing, then, is the vision Mother Church holds out to us in the council documents. How soberly, too, ought we to heed the prophetic summons of which she speaks:

---

[12] Frank Sheed, *Death into Life: A Conversation* (New York: Arena Lettres, 1977), 92.
[13] *Death into Life*, 92.

"For when Christ shall appear and the glorious resurrection of the dead will take place, the glory of God will light up the heavenly City and the Lamb will be the lamp thereof. Then the whole Church of the saints in the supreme happiness of charity will adore God and 'the Lamb who was slain,' proclaiming with one voice: 'To Him who sits upon the throne, and to the Lamb blessing, and honor, and glory, and dominion forever and ever.'"[14]

---

[14] Second Vatican Council, *Lumen Gentium*, no. 51.

CHAPTER XII

GIVING LIFE
TO THE GEEKS

In *Confessions of a Twentieth-Century Pilgrim*, his published account of events urging him along the road to Rome, the late Malcolm Muggeridge recalls the actual day on which he and his beloved wife, Kitty, were received into the Catholic Church. It was at the Chapel of Our Lady Help of Christians, situated in some obscure Sussex village, that the ceremony took place. The bishop of Arundel was there, along with two other priests, one of whom brought a number of children with Down's syndrome in tow, whose noisy presence at first awakened feelings of alarm ("I foresee the children fidgeting, moving about, emitting strange sounds."). But, in fact, says Muggeridge, "quite unexpectedly and mysteriously," a profound sense of peace took hold, "transforming what might otherwise be a respectable quiet ceremony into an unforgettable spiritual experience."[1]

In thinking over what had happened afterwards, Muggeridge suddenly realized that such genetic "misfits," whom the world has come more and more to discard, so affronted are we by their obvious imperfections, were in fact denizens of another world. With their celestial origin, their mission to this world and its self-satisfied inhabitants was, he believed, "to make outward and visible the physical and mental distortions which we all have inwardly and

---

[1] Malcolm Muggeridge, *Confessions of a Twentieth-Century Pilgrim* (San Francisco: Harper & Row Publishers, 1988), 11.

invisibly."[2] In other words, in the absence of such conspicu-
ously deformed specimens, we humans might well suppose
ourselves to be perfectly formed beings. And indeed among
simpler societies, Muggeridge noted, it was precisely the
ones *not* up to scratch, for example, the paralytic and
imbecilic, who were the most revered members. We, of
course, steeped in pseudosophistication, pronounce them
handicapped, "and persuade ourselves that by murdering
them all before or just after they are born, the norm, the
model ad-man with his everlasting smile exposing his
perfect teeth, will become Everyman."[3]

So Muggeridge and his wife, by God's good grace,
effected their entry into a Church encompassed by cripples
on every side; not the beautiful people, certainly, but the
lame and the unlovely, whom only a wounded and outcast
Christ could possibly love. The experience, he later said in
a summary as moving and profound as anything he ever
wrote, imparted to each of them "[a] sense of homecoming,
of picking up the threads of a lost life, of responding to a bell
that had long been ringing, of taking a place at a table that
had long been vacant."[4] Yes, a table that had long been
vacant but was now crowded with such leprous and lost
souls as Jesus Himself had found—like Kitty and Malcolm
Muggeridge, who were only too delighted to be asked to find
a place at God's table.

"Why are you always writing about freaks?" It was a
question often put to Flannery O'Connor, whose wonderful stories are filled with them. Why is there this penchant
for the diseased and demented which seems so peculiarly a

---

[2] *Confessions of a Twentieth-Century Pilgrim*, 11.
[3] *Confessions of a Twentieth-Century Pilgrim*, 12.
[4] *Confessions of a Twentieth-Century Pilgrim*, 13.

trait of southern writers? "[B]ecause we are still able to recognize one," she answered. "To be able to recognize a freak,
you have to have some conception of the whole man, and
in the South the general conception of man is still, in the
main, theological."[5] While the South, she thought, was
hardly a Christ-centered region, with its citizenry steeped in
the things of God, it was nevertheless Christ-haunted.
"The Southerner, who isn't convinced of it, is very much
afraid that he may have been formed in the image and
likeness of God"[6]—hence the centrality of the freak in
Southern literature as a convenient symbol for that "essential displacement"[7] (she called it) which marks our status in
a fallen universe. In other words, we must all appear pretty
freakish in the sight of God, whose bird's-eye view of our
brokenness is the only perspective that finally matters.

None of us is exempt from membership in a fallen race;
thus a living sense of loss, of universal privation, ought to
inform all our actions. It is only in ages intoxicated by the
myth of progress, of man's inexorable perfectibility, that
men seek to rid the world of the misfit, the "handicapped,"
and the moron. Because they prevent our thinking the
world a perfect place, we resent the reminder of its abiding
imperfection that they carry. And where else but at Mass is
that reminder more insistent or intrusive? Where else but
among the churchgoing do we confront, with irritating reg-
ularity, the most hideous examples of humankind disfigured
by sin? Certainly it is not among the country club set, with
its stern ethos of exclusivity, that one is likely to come across

---

[5] Flannery O'Connor, *Mystery and Manners* (New York: Farrar, Straus &
Giroux, 1969), 44.
[6] *Mystery and Manners*, 44-45.
[7] *Mystery and Manners*, 45.

the wretched of the earth; nor, within its tonier precincts, is it any likelier that evidence will be shown of the hidden fault line running through the membership list. Oh, it is there all right, but hardly the sort of thing people of style would advertise; in fact, they may not even be aware of it themselves. As Chesterton used to say, "Men can always be blind to a thing so long as it is big enough."[8] No, it is only the People of God that may boast of the great unwashed, its ranks replete with the most rotten and wayward of men. Why else did Christ suffer to fashion this People if not to deliver it from a myriad of afflictions? He surely did not come for those who think themselves well enough not to need redeeming. Or, rather, He did, but not until they are disposed to accept His diagnosis of their desperate state can it do them any good. Blessed be, therefore, not the chic, but the geek, for he alone can be moved by God's grace His glory to seek.

This was, I will confess, most vividly brought home to me years ago in Saigon, shortly before its collapse and surrender to the victorious North Vietnamese, who straightaway turned the place into a concentration camp called Ho Chi Minh City. I was a mere conscript of the American army at the time, armed with a jeep and a typewriter in the event of an invasion. On Sunday mornings I would drive a kindly old chaplain to say Mass at the once beautiful cathedral church built a hundred years ago by the then-occupying French, who first colonized Indochina. In order actually to get into the building, one had to navigate one's way past a surging sea of human refuse—derelict old men, soldiers without limbs, refugee women and children, their thin outstretched

---

[8] G. K. Chesterton, *The Superstition of Divorce* (London: Chatto & Windus, 1920), 100.

arms pathetically eager to take whatever coins the faithful on its way to holy Mass might toss their way. So this was the anteroom to God's house, I thought to myself, hardly the rich vestibule of suburban Catholicism I was accustomed to growing up in affluent America surrounded by well-scrubbed worshippers dressed for success. And my job, I soon realized, was to part with as much of my money as was humanly decent before going in, and never to scorn as unworthy or beneath contempt a single one of those miserable beggars, for had not God gone about disguised as one of these? Had not my namesake, Martin of Tours, also a soldier, split his cloak in two lest a poor man freeze, only to encounter Christ in a dream adorned in the same mantle of misery? How could one presume to enter God's dwelling place, there to worship in spirit and truth, without first acknowledging Him in such dolorous disguise outside? "Whose is this horrifying face," asks the poet David Gascoyne,

This putrid flesh, discolored, flayed,
Fed on by flies, scorched by the sun?[9]

We needn't look very far to find Him, says Gascoyne. "Behold the Man: He is Man's Son."[10] And He will remain in agony, our agony which, in becoming man He took on, until the world's end. How wide then must the wounds of that world be, if Christ Himself be encircled, pierced by its pain?

---

[9] David Gascoyne, "Ecce Homo," in *Poems, 1937-1942* (London: Nicholson and Watson, 1943). See also *The Faber Book of Religious Verse* (London: Faber and Faber, 1972).
[10] Gascoyne, "Ecce Homo."

"We think that Paradise and Calvary," declares John Donne,

Christ's Cross and Adam's tree, stood in one place;
Look Lord, and find both Adams met in me;
As the first Adam's sweat surrounds my face,
May the last Adam's blood my soul embrace.[11]

Or, to put the thought in yet more rhapsodic form, look at that unsurpassed sacramentalist of the nineteenth century, Gerard Manley Hopkins, giving exultant expression to the fact that, in God's eye, we are all one in the Son, Jesus Christ:

. . . For Christ plays in ten thousand places,
Lovely in limbs, and lovely in eyes not his
To the Father through the features of men's faces.[12]

Faces, alas, not always so lovely to look upon: That, I now see, became the singular experience I had of the Vietnam War. It was, I now realize, about the only lesson I managed to salvage from a struggle that otherwise sundered my country in two. Here, outside the Catholic Mass, were people whom God had taken such trouble to redeem, who belonged, therefore, on the inside, in order precisely to complete that symbolism of solidarity first struck by Christ Himself when, nailed to the Cross, He entered entirely into the world's pain and loss. Unless the war was about

---

[11] John Donne, "Hymn to God, my God, in my Sickness," in *The Complete Poetry of John Donne* (Garden City, N.Y.: Doubleday & Company, 1967), 391.

[12] Gerard Manley Hopkins, "'As kingfishers catch fire, dragonflies draw flame,'" in *The Poems of Gerard Manley Hopkins*, 4th ed. (London: Oxford University Press, 1967), 90.

defending *their* right, the right of the indigent and imbecil-ic to protection from the U.S. flag, then it was no longer worthwhile our trying to win it. It had become a matter of seeing life either as an anthill or the Mystical Body, and if it were only an anthill then why the hell make sacrifices for this or that specimen, there being nothing of value to endear us to anyone? One would make sacrifices only because, to quote the Lady Julian of Norwich, "[I]n the sight of God all of mankind is one man, and one man is all of mankind."[13] Here was the only possible first principle of political life. It came to me as a sort of sunburst upon see-ing, Sunday after Sunday, so endless an array of life loved by God. Only the truth of the brotherhood of man rooted in the Fatherhood of God was worth the agony and the sweat. And who but Mother Church, matrix of a renewed humanity, to choose an image beloved by the Church Fathers, possesses the key to that promised fraternity? She is open to all who come to her; her members may be drawn from anywhere and everywhere, be they rich or poor, bright or dim, whole or crippled. Her task, like the shape of the colonnade at St. Peter's in Rome, is to embrace the entire world. Henri de Lubac reminds us, "By virtue of the divine power received from her Founder, the Church is an institu-tion which endures; but even more than an institution, she is a life that is passed on. She sets the seal of unity on all the children of God whom she gathers together."[14]

---

[13] Juliana of Norwich, *Revelations of Divine Love* (Garden City, N.Y.: Doubleday & Company, 1977), 166.

[14] Henri Cardinal de Lubac, S.J., *The Splendor of the Church* (San Francisco: Ignatius Press, 1986), 54.

There was another vignette that powerfully engraved itself upon my mind. The story was once told to me of a priest who witnessed Francis Xavier saying Mass. It was over four centuries ago, in India, and at this Mass there sat row upon row of lepers waiting to receive God. The priest, fairly shaken by the sight, horrified even by wave upon wave of human wretchedness, evidently hung fire when the saintly missionary gestured to him to come forward and help distribute Holy Communion. But moved by some secret grace, he was able at last to overcome his native repugnance, and the story happily ended with the priest pushing resolutely toward the teeming lepers to bring them God. That, it has always seemed to me, marks the deepest meaning of the Incarnation. Not only does God deliver us from the muck and the mire of sin—not only does He venture forth in mad, passionate search of sinners—but He Himself also descended into that muck and mire, becoming that very sin, the scourge and curse of God Almighty, in order to reconcile the world to God! It is an amazement no greater than which can be imagined.

If Christianity be true, and if the Sacrifice of the Mass be the crucible in which that truth is tested and confirmed day after day, then surely it is a religion in which every human being who ever existed, however twisted or deformed the configuration of its basic humanity, is intended by God for inclusion within the grace of Christ, the very Household of God's Body, the Church. Here is the clearest teaching of the Second Vatican Council, resoundingly set forth in the pivotal text from *Gaudium et Spes*, about which John Paul II has often spoken with unmatched eloquence: "The truth is that only in the mystery of the incarnate Word does the mystery of man take on light. For Adam, the first man, was a figure of Him Who was to come, namely Christ the Lord.

Christ, the final Adam, by the revelation of the mystery of the Father and His love, fully reveals man to man himself and makes his supreme calling clear."[15]

Suffer the little children to come unto me, Jesus tells us (cf. Mk. 10:14). Had He substituted lunatic and cripple, would one whit of meaning of His message have been sacrificed? Who more than they evince greater helplessness in a world harnessed to strength? We live in a world where a man's worth is judged by his work, by what he can do. And what do powerless people do besides consume great quantities of food, water, and space that others provide? Is it possible, however, to see their brokenness as proof of God's love for the world—proof even that He will not destroy the world for its manifold wickedness, so long as it suffers the weak to come unto Him? "Because of these helpless beings," He tells us (as it were), "I have held my wrath in check. These favored few are most peculiarly the object of My love; My heart beats especially for them." And thus the world is spared such destruction as its iniquities deserve.

Finally, there is this description from the pen of the greatest American storyteller of the nineteenth century, Nathaniel Hawthorne. One day, visiting a workhouse in Liverpool, a particularly loathsome-looking child takes a sudden and strange fancy to him, fully expecting to be picked up by the distant and fastidious Hawthorne. It was, said Hawthorne, "as if God had promised the child this favor on my behalf." He could not decently refuse. "I should never have forgiven myself if I had repelled his advances." And so, summoning all the reserves of his heart despite the

---

[15] Second Vatican Council, Pastoral Constitution on the Church in the Modern World *Gaudium et Spes* (December 7, 1965), no. 22.

accumulated ancestral ice of Puritan New England, the noble Hawthorne condescended to pick up the child and hold him in his arms, and caress him, he says, "as tenderly as if he had been its father."[16]

Years later, his daughter Rose, destined to become a famous foundress of an order of sisters charged with caring for the cancerous poor, would conclude that her father's account seemed to her to contain the greatest words he ever wrote. In God's eyes, the geeks and the freaks are truly the world's beautiful people. He suffers them to come unto Him in holy Church, where, in mysterious smallness and insignificance, He dwells. Who can refuse so blithe an invitation from God?

---

[16] Nathaniel Hawthorne, as quoted by Flannery O'Connor in her superb collection of essays, *Mystery and Manners*, 217-19.

CHAPTER XIII

HOMAGE TO THE QUEEN MOTHER

There is only one thing, one reform, that will rescue the world from ruin. And it is not politics, the practice of which in the 1990s has raised reptilian ethics to the highest reaches of our national life. Nor is it, to the astonishment of those fixated on dreams of avarice, the idols of money and material prosperity. The so-called money people, whose ranks are filled with both hard-bitten conservatives urging business to make more and harebrained liberals wanting government to spend more, cannot possibly assuage the hungers of the human heart.

In short, there are no solutions to the mess we find ourselves in. To pretend that proposals possessing liberal or conservative inflection will, like some tribal talisman passed around the campfire, succeed in overcoming the malaise gripping this country, is to evince the very symptoms of the dis-ease we need to rid ourselves of. Only we cannot pull it off. However much of the world may be seduced by riches, or blinded by power, neither politics nor business is the answer. Only the witness of sanctity can save us now. Nothing less will deliver the world from the moral chaos into which it seems to be in headlong descent. Holiness alone is the fulcrum on which the rebuilding of a ruined world will have to depend.

Have you noticed how, in a collapsing social order, one's choices become terrifyingly simple? Just when the center seems no longer to hold and, quoting Marshall Berman on modernity, "all that is solid melts into air,"[1] our precious human liberty has got to decide: gangsterism or God? Do I turn to thuggery or transcendence? Indeed, in this strangely neo-Augustinian time in which we live, an age marked by the spreading violence and chaos of disintegrating structures, more and more of us will be forced to choose (as Augustine well knew) between loving God even to the exclusion of self, or loving self even to the exclusion of God. *Caritas* versus *cupiditas* (charity verses cupidity).[2] There is no third way.

"I proclaim no facile apocalyptic,"[3] writes Romano Guardini at the close of *The End of the Modern World*, a haunting work written in the aftermath of the destruction of Nazi Germany, which my old friend and mentor Fritz Wilhelmsen, on first introducing it to this country in the old Regnery edition, wisely predicted would "cauterize the spirit"[4] of any man who reads it. "For Romano Guardini writes of the end of our world. And he writes of the world which is to come."[5]

"No man has the right to say that the End is here," says Guardini, "for Christ Himself has declared that only the Father knows the day and the hour (Mt. 24:36). If we speak here of the nearness of the End, we do not mean nearness in the sense of time, but nearness as it pertains to the essence

---

[1] Marshall Berman, *All That Is Solid Melts into Air* (New York: Viking Penguin, 1988).

[2] Cf. Saint Augustine, *The City of God*, in *Nicene and Post-Nicene Fathers*, 1st ser., vol. 2, ed. Philip Schaff (Peabody, Mass.: Hendrickson Publishers, 1994), bk. XIV, chap. 28.

[3] Rev. Romano Guardini, *The End of the Modern World: A Search for Orientation* (New York: Sheed & Ward, 1956), 133.

[4] *The End of the Modern World*, 13.

[5] *The End of the Modern World*, 3.

of the End, for in essence man's existence is now nearing an absolute decision. Each and every consequence of that decision bears within it the greatest potentiality and the most extreme danger."[6]

The choices are these: either the Mystical Body of Christ or the anthill. Take your pick. Heaven knows, we've seen quite enough of the one; perhaps it is time to try the other. And when enough people fall to their knees, their minds undistracted by a depraved culture, their hearts set on the God and Father of Jesus Christ, then the world may be lifted once more onto the plane of glory.

Who, then, better than God's Holy Mother—our Mother—is there to show us the way? "Him whom the heavens cannot contain, the womb of one woman bore," exclaimed Saint Augustine. "She ruled our Ruler; she carried Him in Whom we are; she gave milk to our Bread."[7] How extraordinary the paradox by which we are saved. Who else but the woman whose very name, Theotokos, bespeaks salvation, is so singularly situated to impart it to us, nurturing us all the way home to Heaven?

And to think that she might not have made it onto the pages of Lumen Gentium at all. The decision of the council was rather close, the merest majority voting not to issue a separate treatise on Mary but rather to insert her into the larger life of the Church. She is, after all, the Mother of the Church, to cite the title which Paul VI, in his closing allocution on November 21, 1964, the day *Lumen Gentium* was promulgated, actually conferred upon her.

---

[6] *The End of the Modern World*, 133.
[7] Saint Augustine, *Sermon 184*, in *St. Augustine: Sermons for Christmas and Epiphany*, trans. Thomas Comerford Lawler (Westminster, Md.: The Newman Press, 1952), 75.

What else are we to do with her? She belongs both to Christ and to ourselves; the Redeemer to Whom she remains uniquely joined, and the redeemed of whom she remains the most perfect example. "*O filia del tuo figlio!*"[8] is how Dante put it in words of incomparable lyric beauty. "O daughter of your son!"

What, in any case, can her mediation mean, that is, the superb and mysterious title affixed by Sacred Tradition concerning her role as Mediatrix, unless it includes this profound availability of grace poured out upon the world through her? And, moreover, because she remains the Mother of her Son, our Savior Jesus Christ, is she not Coredemptrix also, insofar as her entire being exists in the most intimate, unique, and unsurpassed cooperation with His Redemption of the world?

In Mary, the whole life of the Church, the pilgrim People of God, is hollowed out, prefigured in purest perfection. Both contour and completion, seed and fullness, Mary possesses in ageless splendor all that the Church pines to possess at the end of the age, on the other side of history. As each of us struggles painfully to reach the pinnacle of grace, the promised glory of paradise, Mother Mary already occupies the topmost stair, whence she intercedes on behalf of sinners everywhere. How can this be? Because in the Church, as Cardinal Journet reminds us, "Our Lady alone is more than the whole Church itself."[9] Until we admit, in other words, the Church's true beginnings amid the silence of Mary's heart, freshly awakened by the visitation of an

---

[8] Dante Alighieri, *Paradiso*, in *La Divina Commedia*, canto 33, line 1.
[9] Charles Cardinal Journet, *Les Sept Paroles du Christ en Croix* (n.p., n.d.), 63, quoted in Henri Cardinal de Lubac, S.J., *The Splendor of the Church* (San Francisco: Ignatius Press, 1986), 342.

angel in that little room in Nazareth, we shan't have a clue as to the nature or destiny of an institution called Roman Catholicism. "She is 'Church' right from the start," writes Balthasar, "because she is dispossessed: she is the Church's most interior, most purified reality, a reality that always remains fundamental, however many-all-too human and questionable layers are built on top, superstructures that always stand in need of reformation."[10]

Mary, to whom the Fathers of the Church freely applied the language of Ephesians, not hesitating to designate her as the new Israel, the Bride most holy and immaculate, luminously beautiful (cf. Eph. 5:27)—Mary does not stand in need of the least reformation. Thus from the sheer overflowing spring of her abundant life, deriving directly from an unheard of spousal relation to the Spirit, an entire world is vouchsafed the hope of lasting joy. "If the Church is the Temple of God," writes Henri de Lubac in a breathtaking exposition of the patristic sources, "Mary is the sanctuary of that Temple; if the Church is that sanctuary, Mary is within it, as the Ark was. And if the Church herself be compared to the Ark, then Our Lady is the Propitiatory, more precious than all else, which covers it. If the Church is paradise, Our Lady is the spring from which flows the river that waters it."[11]

In short, our Mother Mary is all that makes glad the City of God. What better way for God to blaze the trail through the world's body than through her who bore the whole mystery of our salvation in her own body? The very one in

---

[10] Rev. Hans Urs von Balthasar, *You Crown the Year with Your Goodness: Radio Sermons* (San Francisco: Ignatius Press, 1989), 196.

[11] De Lubac, *The Splendor of the Church*, 352-53, citations omitted.

whose womb the great wedding of God's Word to the world first took place, the first kiss of the Word becoming the pledge of an unending intimacy, is surely qualified to lead the race back to the Father. Let us heed the inspired words of Saint Gregory the Great, who, in pondering the mystery of Christ's coming, duly noted that "the Father made a marriage feast for his Son by joining the Church to [H]im through the mystery of his incarnation. The womb of the Virgin who bore him was the bridal chamber of this bridegroom."[12] Is that not the whole meaning of her virginal and maternal role, her mysterious mediation— her advocacy, no less!—namely, to draw all men back to Him, her Son, Who is our Savior and Brother?

How beautifully the poet Hopkins puts it in his superb lyric, "The Blessed Virgin Compared to the Air We Breathe." His theme, borne aloft by the title, is a veritable hymn of praise to Our Lady, the circumambient Mother ("Wild air, world-mothering air, / Nestling me everywhere"[13]), whose mantle of grace extends to the four winds, encompassing the whole of creation. He writes:

> This air, which, by life's law,
> My lung must draw and draw
> Now but to breathe its praise,
> Minds me in many ways
> Of her who not only
> Gave God's infinity

---

[12] Saint Gregory the Great, *Homily 38*, in *Gregory the Great: Forty Gospel Homilies*, trans. Dom David Hurst (Kalamazoo: Cistercian Publications, 1990), 341.

[13] Rev. Gerard Manley Hopkins, S.J., "The Blessed Virgin Compared to the Air We Breathe," in *The Poems of Gerard Manley Hopkins*, 4th ed. (London: Oxford University Press, 1967), 93.

Dwindled to infancy
Welcome in womb and breast,
Birth, milk, and all the rest
But mothers each new grace
That does now reach our race—
Mary Immaculate.[14]

She is the one, says Hopkins, who "This one work has to do— / Let all God's glory through."

I say that we are wound
With mercy round and round
As if with air: the same
Is Mary, more by name.
She, wild web, wondrous robe,
Mantles the guilty globe,
Since God has let dispense
Her prayers His providence:
Nay, more than almoner,
The sweet alms' self is her
And men are meant to share
Her life as life does air.[15]

There exists a charming and instructive tradition in the Church, whose origins trace at least as far back as Tertullian, according to which our blessed Lord died on the Cross exactly thirty-three years following His conception by the Holy Spirit in the womb of the Virgin Mary. In other words, by a most extraordinary convergence of calendar dates, which only God Himself would seem clever enough to contrive, both the feast of the Annunciation and the event of the Cross fall on the same day.

---

[14] "The Blessed Virgin Compared to the Air We Breathe," 94.
[15] "The Blessed Virgin Compared to the Air We Breathe," 94-95.

And of course the striking feature about this, the single fact surrounding this miracle of divine conjunction, is that Mary was there, present at both Christ's Conception and His Cross. Is it not astonishing that she remains equally and indisputably present, both at the very beginning when the Word took flesh, and at the very end when that same flesh was crucified, His Spirit descending into the silence of Sheol?

What can this mean? Certainly it cannot be mere coincidence or happenstance. God does not act randomly in a world in which the drama of His Creation, Redemption, and Sanctification is somehow reduced to a series of fortuitously executed events, the course of their unfolding entirely subject to caprice or accident. That is hardly the mind of Almighty God. Pursuant to the world's salvation, every detail of the drama has already been orchestrated in advance by the Three-Personed God, Who, having authored the script, is surely entitled to act alone in its execution.

But not altogether alone. Astonishingly, the success of the Son's saving mission is made to depend upon the consent of a single human being, in whose hands the fate of the universe will literally hang. And she remains free, utterly free, to refuse. This singular creature of God, this luminous reed of the Spirit, is at liberty to sing whatever song she pleases; she cannot be made to sing the canticle of the Lord, even if in magnifying Him, her spirit too will soar. And so all eternity trembles before the unforced fiat of the woman whose submission to grace may only be asked, never coerced—no, not even to secure our salvation.

Of course, in saying yes to God, Mary finds true freedom; her dispossession of self becomes the source of an undreamed of self-possession. As a result, her life assumes a purity of transparence so powerful that in the future all grace courses through her. "Surrender to God," writes Gertrude von Le Fort, "is the only absolute power that the creature possesses."[16] No creature's surrender has ever been so complete, so profound, so fruitful as that of the Blessed Mother—or so faith-filled. Balthasar tells us, "Faith is the surrender of the entire person: because Mary from the start surrendered everything, her memory was the unsullied tablet on which the Father, through the Spirit, could write His entire Word."[17]

The Marian dimension of the Church, John Paul II has reminded us in his wonderful apostolic letter *Mulieris Dignitatem*, takes place entirely before there is any institution of the Petrine office. Yet it exists without in any way seeking to undermine or even inconvenience the exercise of that very necessary office. Nevertheless, says the pope, "Mary Immaculate precedes all others, including obviously Peter himself and the Apostles. This is so, not only because Peter and the Apostles, being born of the human race under the burden of sin, form part of the Church which is 'holy from out of sinners,' but also because their triple function has no other purpose except to form the Church in line with the ideal of sanctity already programmed and prefigured in Mary. A contemporary theologian has rightly stated that

---

[16] Gertrude von Le Fort, *The Eternal Woman*, trans. Marie Cecilia Buehrle (Milwaukee: Bruce Publishing Company, 1954), 14.

[17] In the sheer nuptial self-surrender that marks the perfection of Mary's faith, we are thus to see her as the personification of that Church already made present before even the apostles were appointed to office. Indeed, in virtue of her fiat, the consent binding her forever to God, the Word is able to take complete possession of her body and soul, in order that she "becomes womb and bride and mother of the incarnating God himself." See *The von Balthasar Reader*, trans. Robert J. Daly and Fred Lawrence, ed. Medard Kehl and Werner Löser (Edinburgh: T. & T. Clark, 1985), 214.

Mary is 'Queen of the Apostles without any pretensions to apostolic powers: she has other and greater powers.'"[18]

The whole point, after all, of the institutional Church—indeed, the reason for all the machinery of office, however poorly or ponderously it grinds—is to bring about the sanctification of its members, to make us more and more like Mary, who shows us what prodigies of grace God can perform in a soul wholly disposed to receive His largess. It is from her perspective, her memory steeped in the things of God, that we need to look and see the wonders wrought by her and God's Son. "It is only in Heaven," Balthasar predicts, "that we shall appreciate how much the Church owes to Mary in understanding the faith." But for now, he adds, "by the fact that she shows herself, she already leads us into the mystery of what the Church is in her essential nature: a pure work of God's grace . . . Our eyes are bleary and dull," he concludes, "we must put on Mary's spectacles in order to see exactly."[19]

I give Hopkins the last word. From the final lines of his incomparable poem, he writes exultantly, beseechingly, of God's Mother, and ours too:

> Stir in my ears, speak there
> Of God's love, O live air,
> Of patience, penance, prayer:
> World-mothering air, air wild,
> Wound with thee, in thee isled,
> Fold home, fast fold thy child.[20]

---

[18] Pope John Paul II, Apostolic Letter on the Dignity and Vocation of Women on the Occasion of the Marian Year *Mulieris Dignitatem* (August 15, 1988), no. 27, n. 55.

[19] Rev. Hans Urs von Balthasar, *Mary for Today* (Middlegreen, Slough, England: St. Paul Publications, 1987), 42, 43, 44.

[20] Hopkins, "The Blessed Virgin Compared to the Air We Breathe," 97.

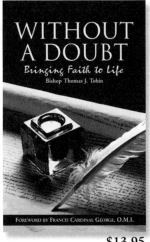